PENGUIN BOOKS

AUSTRALIAN BALLADS

Australia's songs and ballads grew as swiftly as her history. They did not record all of that history, but certain aspects of the young and vast country's traditions, legends, true and tall stories are expressed in the ballads with a simplicity and zest not to be found elsewhere. Dr Russel Ward, author of *The Australian Legend*, is an expert in the subject who has collected many old bush songs and ballads himself. From the vast amount of material available he has made a selection which shows all its liveliness and variety, from old anonymous convict and bushranging songs and ballads to the literary ballads of *The Bulletin* to modern verse in the ballad tradition. In his introduction he has tackled the thorny subject of the composition of many of the ballads, and justified his use of the word 'ballad' to cover all the different types of work he has included in this book. But authorship or questions of category have had little to do with the immense popularity of many of these ballads. 'Bold Jack Donahoe', 'The Wild Colonial Boy', 'Waltzing Matilda' and 'The Man from Snowy River' are as much a part of Australia as is the River Murray; but as well as these Dr Ward has included many others, which like lesser creeks and billabongs are no less refreshing.

Cover from a wood engraving by 'J.D.' from a painting by Samuel Calbert in the National Library, Canberra.

The Penguin Book of

AUSTRALIAN BALLADS

❧

EDITED AND
INTRODUCED BY
RUSSEL WARD

PENGUIN BOOKS

Penguin Books Australia Ltd,
487 Maroondah Highway, P.O. Box 257
Ringwood, Victoria, 3134, Australia
Penguin Books Ltd,
Harmondsworth, Middlesex, England
Penguin Books,
625 Madison Avenue, New York, N.Y. 10022, U.S.A.
Penguin Books Canada Ltd,
2801 John Street, Markham, Ontario, Canada
Penguin Books (N.Z.) Ltd,
182-190 Wairau Road, Auckland 10, New Zealand

First published by Penguin Books Australia, 1964
Reprinted 1967, 1971, 1974, 1978, 1981

This collection Copyright © Penguin Books Australia Ltd, 1964
Introduction Copyright © Russel Ward, 1964

Typeset in Monotype Times Roman

Made and printed in Hong Kong by
Wah Cheong Printing Press Ltd

CIP

The Penguin book of Australian ballads.

First published: Melbourne: Penguin, 1964.
Includes index.
ISBN 0 14 070009 9.

1. Ballads, Australian. I. Ward, Russel, 1914-.

A821'.04408

Contents

5

CONTENTS

II The Gold Rush: New Chums and Diggers (1851-61)

III Settling Down: Early Traditional Bush Ballads (1861-85)

IV Early Literary Balladists (1861-85)

V Traditional Bush Ballads (1885-1914)

VI Literary Bush Ballads (1885-1914)

CONTENTS

VII Town Ballads (1870-   )

CONTENTS

CONTENTS

Acknowledgements

Grateful acknowledgements for permission to reprint verse contained in this volume are made to all living poets whose work appears; to Mr J. R. Skemp, Mrs P. M. Shaw, Mr E. H. Murphy and Mrs H. I. Tierney; to the periodicals *Overland*, *Australian Book Review*, *The Bulletin*, and *Meanjin*; and to Angus & Robertson Ltd, Allan & Co Ltd (Holder of the World Copyright for 'Waltzing Matilda'), Melbourne University Press, the Lothian Publishing Co Ltd, and Edwards & Shaw.

In a small number of cases we have been unable to trace the copyright holders and would appreciate any advice on omissions.

Introduction

SINCE no two people have identical tastes, no editor of an anthology can hope to please much anyone but himself. Every critic, if not every reader, will think of favourite verses which have been omitted, and will accordingly damn the editor for not having had the taste to compile the best possible collection – the one, of course, which the critic would have compiled himself. An editor cannot compile *n* different anthologies (where *n* stands for the number of potential readers), but he can and should explain the principles on which he made his selection.

First then, in the title of this book the accent should be placed on *Australian* rather than on *ballads*. The verses have been chosen primarily to give the flavour of whatever is distinctive, or characteristic or 'typical' of the historical experience of Australians, and so of Australian attitudes to life. But we must stress at once that the 'typical' Australian is not at all the same person as the average Australian, any more than is the 'typical' American, or Frenchman, or Englishman identical with the actual average specimen of his nation. The 'typical' representative of a nation is, necessarily, he who differs most obviously from the average, cosmopolitan European type. How else can a national identity or image be established than by emphasizing those traits which distinguish men of one country from those of another? Certainly not by emphasizing the more numerous traits which all English-speaking peoples or all Europeans, or even all men, hold in common. All Australians are not in fact easy-going, improvident, good mates banded together against affectation and propriety, any more than all Americans are rugged individualists separately thrusting their ways from Log Cabin to White House – or to an industrial tycoon-ship: but, because of the differing historical experience of the two peoples, these differing stereotypes or self-images tend to be recognized by each, and by foreigners – even if ruefully in some cases.

The verses in this book have been chosen, then, because of the light they throw on this Australian self-image and on the historical experience which created it. Most of them are about the bush, the outback – the frontier, in American terminology. Again, we must stress that this does not mean that the *average* Australian is, or ever was, a wild colonial boy more at home in the saddle than the salon. In fact over two-thirds of Australians today live in, or very near, the great capital cities and a higher proportion of Australians have always been city-dwellers than in almost any other country. It does mean that – at any rate sixty years ago when the bush ballads were most popular – most Australians admired the bushman's characteristics, as portrayed in the ballads and elsewhere, partly because these characteristics were felt to be peculiarly Australian: as indeed they were in the sense that they necessarily diverged most widely from British norms. It was much easier to preserve traditional British manners and mental attitudes in a Sydney or Adelaide suburban street, than it was a thousand miles inland in a bark hut on the Barcoo River (which flows perhaps once in six years). So much then for the interpretation placed on the word *Australian* in the book's title. What of the word *Ballads*?

At one time or another it has been used to cover an astonishingly wide range of verse, but in its narrower sense most people now use it to mean narrative folk-verse, or narrative literary verse written in the style of folk-ballads. In this sense most, though by no means all, of the poems in this book are ballads: but to help build up a picture of the traditional Australian self-image, I have not hesitated to include much non-narrative verse of a popular sort. Indeed a more accurately descriptive title might have been the *Penguin Book of Australian Popular Verse*, were it not for the last section which includes some first-rate, but not particularly 'popular', contemporary Australian poems. These have been chosen to suggest the extent to which traditional Australian values, reflected for so long in popular verse, have influenced the inner content, if not the outer style, of our literature and life today.

I have taken it for granted that Australia has a large number of folk-ballads and songs, but there are still some cultivated persons who hold that there is no such thing as a genuine Australian folk-song, in spite of the fact that the most prolific versifier in this book is *Anon*. Such people expound three main arguments, each of which is false in itself and at the same time incompatible with their other two lines of reasoning.

First they examine, say, the verses in Section V, find that they are very different in style and content from traditional British countryside folk-songs, and proclaim that therefore they are not folk-songs at all. On this reasoning American Negro spirituals and other American folk-songs do not exist either. Second, they show that many Australian traditional verses have borrowed their tunes or words or theme from overseas, and argue that therefore, though they may be genuine folk-songs, they are not Australian at all but English or Irish, or even Scottish or American as the case may be. On this reasoning some of the oldest and most thoroughly English and Scottish folk-ballads are also spurious, because they can be shown to have Scandinavian or other continental ancestry. Third, these cultivated critics usually subscribe to the outworn romantic theory which defines folk-song by reference to its origins. An authentic folk-song, it is held, *must* have originated as an anonymous, spontaneous, collective emanation from the common 'folk' gathered, as it were, in committee on the village green. On this assumption, because some Australian folk-songs can be traced back to an original single author, whether a highly literate person or not, it is held that all Australian folk-songs are not genuine folk-material at all.

The truth is that, because Australian history is so short and so recent, it is much easier for the student to trace a folk-song to its source. Even so, most Australian folk-verse remains as bafflingly anonymous as nearly all folk-verse does in older countries. In the minority of cases where it is possible to trace origins, they fall into three main categories. First there are songs which can be positively shown to have sprung, not indeed from a 'folk committee' on the village green, but from one gathered round the camp-fire or shearers' 'huts'. Such a song is *Shearing in the Bar* (Section VI). Of its composition Mr Tritton writes:

Well, that came to me by being up at the Tarcoon pub one afternoon, one Saturday, and I suppose there'd be thirty or forty shearers there from various sheds, and everyone of them was talking about his shearing ... shearing, nothing else. And the point that struck me, nobody seemed to gash them, no matter how rough they were. Well,

I got stuck into that, and I thought: 'Well, that's an idea,' . . . and I made up a story about it in rhyme. At that time, I had no intention of it being sung, but my cobber, Dutchy Bishop, he suggested we put a tune to it, and we tried several, and the one we tried it on was of all things in the world When Irish Eyes Are Smiling . . . Well, it started on that but it got a bit difficult to hit those high notes, and so we chopped it down a bit . . . I take the credit for making it up myself — but when I look back, I had a hell of lot of offsiders! Everybody was putting in a verse or a line here and there: 'Try this,' and 'Try that.' One would have one version and then another would add something else, and so we came to the one that finally developed . . . There were quite a few learnt the song, you know, and they spread it around the country. One time we were having a bit of a session; there was one bloke sang three verses of it and claimed it as his own. And I took exception to that. And there were a few blows exchanged, and he apologized after; and he admitted it wasn't when I sung the other verses to him.

In the nature of things, no such positive demonstration of collective 'folk' composition is likely to be produced for older folksongs in older lands – though to write this admittedly reminds one rather of the discharged mental-hospital patient who boasted that he was the only man in the township with a certificate to *prove* that he was sane. Many more Australian folk-ballads in this first group can only be presumed, like most British traditional ballads, to have begun in such a way.

Second, a good many Australian traditional verses can be shown to have derived from overseas, usually English or Irish, folk-songs. The relationship of the Australian song to its overseas 'original' ranges all the way from close imitation or parody, to a derivation so remote as to be unrecognizable except by the attentive student. A good example of this type is *Like a True-born Native Man* (Section II), which is fairly closely related to a cycle of British folk-songs including *The True-born Irishman* and *The True-born Journeyman*.

Third, there are a number of Australian traditional songs which can be shown to have begun as the individual work of a literary man or popular stage-entertainer. This is not to say, of course, that any or every song of the popular stage ever was, or became, a folk-song. It is to say that a few did. For example, Charles Thatcher (see Section II) composed and sang hundreds of popular and topical songs on the Victorian gold-fields. There is conclusive evidence that a very few of them so tickled the fancy of his audiences that they were learnt by heart, passed on orally from singer to singer, and so changed in the process that not only was their original authorship forgotten, but they became truly composite 'folk' productions. Thatcher's original manuscript version of *The Queer Ways of Australia* survives in the Public Library of Victoria. It has six stanzas and the chorus. Thirty years or so after its composition, a passenger on a Queensland coastal ship wrote down the words (reproduced in Section II) of a 'thoroughly up-country song, well-known in Northern Queensland'. This anonymous version of Thatcher's original has dropped two of its six stanzas. Three of the remaining four remain fairly close to the originals, but the last stanza has been changed and improved almost beyond recognition in the process of oral transmission. The reader may compare the 'folk' version in Section II with this equivalent stanza as it came from Thatcher's pen:

> Now instead of a glass of home-brewed ale
> Every morning he'd not fail
> To sing out for a gin cocktail
>   A favourite drink in Australia.
> He talked away at a fearful rate
> Of nobblers and of brandy straight
> On spiders too he would dilate
> And astonish his poor sister Kate
> He kissed the buxom servant maid
> Nice pranks I tell you he played
> Says he 'My dear don't be afraid
>   It's a way we've got in Australia.'

It is, of course, possible that the last stanza of the 'folk' version derives from a seventh stanza composed by Thatcher but not written down by him in the manuscript. Whether a song of this type should be regarded as a folk-song or not depends upon how far the process of 'folk re-creation' has proceeded, upon how many variant folk-versions have been collected, and upon the 'flavour' of the end-product. The point is that we have no means of proving that some of the Scottish border-ballads, for instance, did not *originate* in the same way – if we substitute a 'professional'

medieval minstrel or court poet for the popular stage enter-
tainer or versifier of the nineteenth century. What we know of
the processes of folk-composition in young countries like Aus-
tralia and the United States makes it likely that similar processes
obtained in older countries hundreds of years earlier.

For these reasons there can usually be no such thing as the
'true', or 'correct', or 'original' version of a folk-song. By com-
parison of a large number of variant versions of a given ballad,
specialist students can often learn much of its origins: but in a
short book like this, addressed to the general reader, it is not
possible to print variant versions together with an account of
the source of each. The versions here published come from a
variety of sources — from my own collection of verses taken down
from the lips of many folk-singers, from manuscripts, and from
other printed versions in old newspapers and modern antho-
logies. Though keenly aware that the decision will be condemned
by many scholars, I have frequently combined elements from
various sources to make a 'composite' version when to do so
makes for greater completeness or dramatic force. This, after all,
is what folk-singers do every time they sing. It goes without
saying, then, that the words of practically every piece of folk-
verse in this book will differ, in at least some degree, from those
which appear under the same titles in other collections.

To say that Australia possesses a considerable body of folk-
verse is not to claim that its poetic (or musical) quality is as high
as that of the best folk-songs of the English or Scottish or Irish
countryside. It is not. Yet we should remember that the best-
known British folk-ballads have been singled out over a long
period of time from a vast mass of mediocre verse and outright
doggerel. It may be too that mere distance in time and space is
responsible for much of the poetic appeal of old-country folk-
songs. Familiarity breeds contempt. What now seems colloquial
and vulgar, or merely banal, may in the future seem naïvely dig-
nified, quaint, and even heroic. One reason why there is now much
more interest in Australian traditional verse than there was
thirty years ago is that its language, its stage-properties and the
way of life it figures forth, is no longer perfectly familiar to the
great majority of Australians. It seems to me quite possible that,

in a few hundred years' time, English-speaking critics may judge *The Old Bullock Dray* quite comparable, as poetry, with *The Wife Wrapt in the Wether's Skin* or *The Death of Ben Hall* with *The Death of Robin Hood*.

However that may be, all who know Australia will agree that both the anonymous and 'literary' verses in this book mirror the popular Australian stance as faithfully, if not always as delicately, as the popular verse of any other country reflects the attitudes received as 'typical' of its people. And after all, Australians have not commonly prided themselves on their delicacy. If the reader remains unconvinced by the necessarily small selection in this book, he is confidently referred to John Manifold's *Penguin Australian Song Book* and to Douglas Stewart and Nancy Keesing's *Old Bush Songs* and *Australian Bush Ballads*.

The verse has been arranged chronologically, but only very loosely so. Just as the book includes much non-ballad verse, provided it helps to body forth the popular Australian self-image of yesterday, so each Section may include some verses composed outside its designated time-span provided such verses throw light on the events and attitudes of the period. For example, many of the poets in Section IV, *Early Literary Balladists*, wrote after Lawson and Paterson had become popular; but they have been placed among the early forerunners because their work reflects an earlier, imperfectly assimilated, 'immigrant' attitude to bush life.

Today, as in the past, there are some refined Australians who do not much like the traditional national attitude to life figured forth in our popular verse. They find the tradition at once naïve, crude, and stultifying, and they plead passionately for a more cosmopolitan and sophisticated set of values. There is something in this argument, of course. The legendary bushman carried in his cultural swag racist delusions and laziness, as well as mateship, and endurance, and a full share of what G. K. Chesterton called 'God's scorn for all men governing.' But he who repudiates his ancestry forfeits the reversion. Among the most sensitive and cultivated living Australians are those whose poetry shows that they, like most of their countrymen, feel no need to disown their inheritance. The best poems in Section VIII show that we can cease to be crude provincials without attempting the impossible task of ceasing to be ourselves.

RUSSEL WARD

University of New England
1964

I

(1788-1851)

EARLY DAYS: CONVICTS, BOLTERS, AND BUSHMEN

IN 1787 King George III's speech to Parliament announced that
'a plan has been formed ... for transporting a number of con-
victs in order to remove the inconvenience which arose from the
crowded state of the gaols.' So Australia was founded on 26
January 1788 when the First Fleet of prisoners and their military
gaolers landed at Sydney Cove. For the first fifty years or so of
its existence 'white' Australia was primarily an increasingly ex-
tensive gaol: but free men, attracted by the booming pastoral
industry, arrived in increasing numbers towards the end of this
period.

The songs and verses which have survived reflect the ways in
which the first arrivals 'settled in' to their new environment. In
Britain, Botany Bay was seen at first satirically, as a remote and
outlandish sink into which could be poured the idle and corrupt
citizens whom their country could well do without. Then came a
number of street or folk-ballads, made in Britain or Australia,
which stressed the loneliness, the home-sickness, and the hard-
ships endured by the involuntary exiles.

Very soon, however, there began to appear other popular
Australian rhymes which took a more light-hearted and realistic
approach to life in the new land. Some convicts 'took to the
bush' as 'bolters' or bushrangers and many more romanticised
their exploits in song. By the 1830s and forties many 'old hands'
(ex-convicts), Currency lads and others had begun to feel at
home in the bush and to look at Australia through native-born
or thoroughly acclimatized eyes. Comparison of the last three
songs in this section with the first three will show how far
acclimatization proceeded in the first seventy years.

ANON

TWO BRITISH STREET-BALLADS

When Australia began, most people in Great Britain and elsewhere were illiterate, and newspapers were few and expensive. In large British cities the function of the modern popular daily press was performed, at least in part, by street-ballads. These 'broadsides' of rhymed doggerel sometimes reproduced old countryside folk-songs, but more often they gave the latest news of the day – in even less accurate and more colourful form than is usual for modern evening newspapers. Murders, rapes, hangings, riots, and victories over foreign foes were the stock-in-trade of the street-ballad monger or 'chaunter', who sold copies of his 'broadsides' for a penny each and sang their contents to passers-by.

These two street-ballads give news – and popular views – of the decision to found Australia as a penal colony. The third-last stanza of the first song refers to William Pitt, the younger, Prime Minister of the day, whose efforts to balance the national budget resulted in a tax on windows and a proposal for taxing shops. 'White Boys', referred to in the second song, were Irish nationalist agitators.

Botany Bay, A New Song

Let us drink a good health to our schemers above,
Who at length have contrived from this land to remove
Thieves, robbers and villains, they'll send 'em away,
To become a new people at Botany Bay.

Some men say they have talents and trades to get bread,
Yet they spunge on mankind to be cloathed and fed,
They'll spend all they get, and turn night into day,
Now I'd have all such sots sent to Botany Bay.

There's gay powder'd coxcombs and proud dressy fops,
Who with very small fortunes set up in great shops,
They'll run into debt with design ne'er to pay,
They should all be transported to Botany Bay.

The tradesman who plays at cards, billiards and dice,
Must pay for their goods an extravagant price,
No faith I'm mistaken such rogues never pay,
Therefore they should all go to Botany Bay.

Many men they are married to good-natur'd wives,
They'll run after wenches and lead debauch'd lives;
Our wise legislature should send such away,
To support their system in Botany Bay.

There's night-walking strumpets who swarms in each street
Proclaiming their calling to each man they meet;
They become such a pest that without delay,
These corrupters of youth should be sent to Botany Bay.

There's monopolisers who add to their store,
By cruel oppression and squeezing the poor,
There's butchers and farmers get rich quick in that way,
But I'd have all such rogues sent to Botany Bay.

We've great men above and gentry below,
They'll talk much of honour, and make a great show,
But yet never think their poor tradesmen to pay,
Such defaulters I'd have sent to Botany Bay.

You lecherous whoremasters who practise vile arts
To ruin young virgins and break parents hearts,
Or from the fond husband the wife leads astray,
Let such debauch'd stallions be sent to Botany Bay.

And that we may sweep our foul nation quite clean,
Send off the shop-tax promoters so mean,
And those who deprive the light of the day,
Should work for a breakfast at Botany Bay.

The hulks and the jails had some thousands in store,
But out of the jails are ten thousand times more,
Who live by fraud, cheating, vile tricks, and foul play,
They should all be sent over to Botany Bay.

Now, should any take umbrage, at what I have writ,
Or here find a bonnet or cap that will fit,
To such I have only this one word to say,
They are all welcome to wear it at Botany Bay.

Botany Bay

Away with these whimsical bubbles of air
Which only excite a momentary stare;
Attention to plans of utility pay,
Weigh anchor, and steer for Botany Bay.

Let no-one think much of a trifling expense,
Who knows what may happen a hundred years hence?
The loss of America what can repay?
New colonies seek for at Botany Bay.

O'er Neptune's domain, how extensive the scope,
Of quickly returning, how defiant the hope.
The Capes must be doubled, and then bear away
Three thousand good leagues to reach Botany Bay.

Of those *precious* souls who for nobody care,
It seems a large cargo the kingdom can spare,
To ship off a gross or two, make no delay,
They cannot too soon go to Botany Bay.

They go of an island to take personal charge,
Much warmer than Britain, and ten times as large,
No custom-house duty, no freightage to pay,
And tax free they live when at Botany Bay.

This garden of Eden, this new promised land,
The time to set sail for will soon be at hand;
Ye worst of land-lubbers make ready for sea,
There's room for you all about Botany Bay.

For a general good make a general sweep,
The beauty of life in good order to keep,
With night-prowling hateful disturbers away,
And send the whole tribe unto Botany Bay.

Ye chiefs who go out on this naval exploit,
The work to accomplish, and set matters right,
To Ireland be kind, call at Cork on your way,
And take some White Boys unto Botany Bay.

Commercial arrangements give prospects of joy,
Fair and firm may be kept every national tie,
And mutual confidence may those who betray
Be sent to the bottom of Botany Bay.

ANON

TWO TRANSPORTATION BALLADS

Many street-ballads were made on the subject of transportation
to 'Botany Bay' (New South Wales) or 'Van Diemen's Land'
(Tasmania). Many, like these two, have survived in innumerable
versions in oral tradition, in Australia as well as in Great Britain.
Most share the sentimental, moralizing tone of *Van Diemen's
Land*. *Farewell to Old England* is actually a popular stage-song
from the 1880s, but it was made over from a more moralistic
street-ballad of the earlier transportation period.

Van Diemen's Land

Come all you gallant poachers that ramble free from care,
That walk out on moonlight nights with your dog, gun and
    snare:
The hares and jolly pheasants you have at your command,
Not thinking that your last career is to Van Diemen's Land.

O there was three men from Galloway town, Brown, Martin
    and Paul Jones.
We was three daring poachers, as the gentry well does know.
One night we was trepanned by the keepers of the land
And fourteen years transported was unto Van Diemen's Land.

The first day that we landed upon that fatal shore,
The planters gathered round us, full twenty score or more;
They ranked us up like horses and sold us out of hand,
And they yok'd us up to ploughs, brave boys, to plough Van
    Diemen's Land.

There was a girl from Dublin Town, Rosanna was her name;
For fourteen years transported was for playing of the game.
Our master bought her freedom and married her out of hand,
And she gave to us good usage upon Van Diemen's Land.

The huts that we must live in are built of sods and clay,
With rotten straw for bedding and we must not say nay.
Our cots are fenced with fire, we slumber when we can,
To fright the dogs and tigers upon Van Diemen's Land.

It's often when in slumber I have a pleasant dream –
A-lying in old Ireland beside a purling stream,
With my true love upon my side and a jug of ale in hand,
But I wake a broken-hearted man all in Van Diemen's Land.

God bless our wives and families, likewise that happy shore,
That isle of great contentment that we shall see no more.
As for our wretched females, see them we seldom can;
There's twenty to one woman upon Van Diemen's Land.

So all you jolly poacher lads, this warning take from me:
I'd have you quit night-walking and to shun bad company,
Throw by your dogs and snares, for to you I speak plain,
For if you knew our hardships you would never poach again.

Farewell to Old England

Farewell to old England for ever,
   Farewell to our rum-culls as well;
Farewell to the well-loved Old Bailey
   Where I used for to cut such a swell.

     Singing too-ra-lie, too-ra-lie, addity,
     Singing too-ra-lie, too-ra-lie, aye,
     Singing too-ra-lie, too-ra-lie, addity,
     We're sailing for Botany Bay.

'Taint leaving Old England we cares about,
   'Taint 'cause we mis-spells what we knows;
But because all we light-fingered gentry
   Hops around with a log on our toes.

There's the captain as is our commandier,
  There's the bosun and all the ship's crew,
There's the first and the second class passengers
  Knows what we poor convicts goes through.

For fourteen long years I'm transported,
  For fourteen long years and a day,
Just for meeting a cove in the alley,
  And stealing his ticker away.

Oh, had I the wings of a turtle-dove!
  I'd soar on my pinions so high;
Slap bang to the arms of my Polly-love
  And in her sweet bosom I'd die.

Now, all you young dukies and duchesses,
  Take warning from what I do say,
Mind, all is your own as you touchesses,
  Or you'll meet us in Botany Bay.

GEORGE CARTER

These famous lines were long believed to have been spoken as the prologue to the first drama produced in Australia, when in 1796 a convict cast performed *The Recruiting Officer* in Sydney Town. The author of the *Prologue* was believed to have been George Barrington (1755-1804), the celebrated pickpocket transported to Sydney in 1791. Actually the *Prologue* was written later as a joke by a Leicester playwright, George Carter, who never set foot in Australia.

True Patriots All

From distant climes, o'er widespread seas we come,
Though not with much *éclat*, or beat of drum;
True patriots all, for be it understood,
We left our country for our country's good:
No private views disgraced our generous zeal,
What urged our travels was our country's weal:
And none will doubt but that our emigration
Has proved most useful to the British nation.
But you inquire, What could our breasts inflame,
With this new passion for theatric fame;
What, in the practice of our former days,
Could shape our talents to exhibit plays?
Your patience, sirs, some observations made,
You'll grant us equal to the scenic trade.
He who to midnight ladders is no stranger,
You'll own will make an admirable Ranger.
To seek Macbeth we have not far to roam,
And sure in Filch I shall be quite at home.
Unrivalled there, none will dispute my claim,
To high pre-eminence and exalted fame.
As oft on Gad's hill we have ta'en our stand,
When 'twas so dark you could not see your hand,
Some true-bred Falstaff, we may hope to start,
Who, when well-bolstered, well will play his part.

The scene to vary, we shall try in time
To treat you with a little pantomime.
Here light and easy Columbines are found,
And well-tried Harlequins with us abound;
From durance vile our precious selves to keep,
We often had recourse to th' flying leap,
To a black face have sometimes ow'd escape,
And Hounslow Heath has proved the worth of crape.
But how, you ask, can we e'er hope to soar
Above these scenes, and rise to tragic lore?
Too oft, alas! we've forced th' unwilling tear,
And petrified the heart with real fear.
Macbeth a harvest of applause will reap,
For some of us, I fear, have murdered sleep;
His lady, too, with grace will sleep and talk
Our females have been used at night to walk.
Sometimes, indeed, so various is our art,
An actor may improve and mend his part;
'Give me a horse,' bawls Richard, like a drone,
We'll find a man would help himself to one.
Grant us your favour, put us to the test,
To gain your smiles we'll do our very best;
And without dread of future Turnkey Tockits,
Thus, in an honest way, still pick your pockets.

ANON

This ballad was published in Australia's first newspaper, the *Sydney Gazette*, of 14 July 1832. By then at least there were many who did not regard Australia as a land of exile. In the early days of the colony there was a great shortage of sterling coinage. Spanish dollars with holes punched in them, notes-of-hand, and other makeshift devices circulated as colonial 'currency' as distinct from sterling. Hence the first generation or so of native-born Australians came to be known as Currency lads and lasses, while those born in Britain were sometimes called 'sterling' people. (For 'Factory', see *Glossary*.)

Botany Bay Courtship

The Currency Lads may fill their glasses
And drink to the health of the Currency Lasses;
But the lass I adore, the lass for me,
Is a lass in the Female Factory.

O! Molly's her name, and her name is Molly,
Although she was tried by the name of Polly;
She was tried and cast for death at Newry,
But the Judge was bribed and so were the Jury.

She got 'death recorded' in Newry town,
For stealing her mistress's watch and gown;
Her little boy Paddy can tell you the tale,
His father was turnkey of Newry jail.

The first time I saw the comely lass
Was at Parramatta, going to mass;
Says I, 'I'll marry you now in an hour,'
Says she, 'Well, go and fetch Father Power.'

But I got into trouble that very same night!
Being drunk in the street I got into a fight,
A constable seized me – I gave him a box –
And was put in the watch-house and then in the stocks.

O! it's very unaisy as I may remember,
To sit in the stocks in the month of December;
With the north wind so hot, and the hot sun right over,
O! sure, and it's no place at all for a lover!

'It's worse than the tread-mill,' says I, 'Mr Dunn,'
'To sit here all day in the hate of the sun!'
'Either that or a dollar,' says he, 'for your folly,' –
But if I had a dollar I'd drink it with Molly.

But now I am out again, early and late
I sigh and I cry at the Factory gate,
'O! Mrs R – – late Mrs F – – n,
'O! won't you let Molly out very soon?'

'Is it Molly McGuigan?' says she to me,
'Is it not?' says I, for she know'd it was she.
'Is it her you mean that was put in the stocks
'For beating her mistress, Mrs Cox?'

'O! yes and it is, madam pray let me in,
'I have brought her a half-pint of Cooper's best gin,
'She likes it as well as she likes her own mother,
'O! now let me in, madam, I am her brother.'

So the Currency Lads may fill their glasses,
And drink to the health of the Currency Lasses;
But the lass I adore, the lass for me,
Is a lass in the Female Factory.

'Frank the Poet' was a convict who composed many popular ballads about the life and outlook of 'Government men' in early Australia. His songs and verses were passed on by oral tradition, often being changed in the process. The next three songs in their original forms, were almost certainly composed by him. The four following ones may have been. Equally, on current evidence, they could have been composed by any number of anonymous folk-singers.

Frank is usually held to have been one Francis McNamara, alias Frank Goddard, born in Dublin in 1758 and transported for uttering forged notes in 1819. He is said to have been incarcerated in the Port Arthur penal settlement in 1842 and to have died about 1853. If so, he must have lived to the age of ninety-five – an almost incredible feat for a convict.

Hearsay records say that he was 'a whimsical and incorrigible scamp' liked by people of all classes, and that he was probably lame. One early source reports that, when he was sailing from Van Diemen's Land for the mainland with a ticket-of-leave, he was called on for an extempore valedictory address. Mounting the steamer's paddle-box, he declaimed:

> 'Land of lags and Kangaroo,
> Of 'possums and the scarce Emu,
> The farmer's pride but the prisoners' Hell.
> Land of Bums, Fare thee well!'

Labouring with the Hoe

I was convicted by the laws of England's hostile crown,
Conveyed across those swelling seas in slavery's fetters bound,
For ever banished from that shore where love and friendship
   grow,
That loss of freedom to deplore and work the labouring hoe.

Despised, rejected and oppressed in tattered rags I'm clad.
What anguish fills my aching breast and almost drives me mad,
When I hear the settler's threatening voice say, 'Arise! to labour go,
Take scourging, convicts, for your choice or work the labouring hoe.'

Growing weary from compulsive toil beneath the noon-tide sun,
While drops of sweat bedew the soil my task remains undone.
I'm flogged for wilful negligence, or the tyrants call it so.
Ah what a doleful recompense for labouring with the hoe.

Behold yon lofty woodbine hills where the rose in the morning shines,
Those crystal brooks that do distil and mingle through those vines,
There seems to be no pleasures gained: they but augment my woe,
Whilst here an outcast doomed to live and work the labouring hoe.

You generous sons of Erin's Isle, whose heart for glory burns,
Pity a wretched exile who his long-lost country mourns.
Restore me heaven to liberty whilst I lie here below,
Untie that clew of bondage and release me from the hoe.

A Convict's Lament on the Death of Captain Logan

I am a native of Erin's island
    But banished now from my native shore;
They tore me from my aged parents,
    And from the maiden I adore.
In transient storms as I set sailing,
    Like mariner bold my course did steer;
Sydney Harbour was my destination –
    That cursed place at length drew near.

I then joined banquet in congratulation
  On my safe arrival from the briny sea;
But, Alas, Alas! I was mistaken –
  Twelve years transportation to Moreton Bay!
Early one morning, as I carelessly wandered,
  By the Brisbane waters I chanced to stray;
I heard a prisoner sadly bewailing,
  Whilst on the sunny river-banks he lay.

He said: 'I've been a prisoner at Port Macquarie,
  At Norfolk Island, and Emu Plains;
At Castle Hill and cursed Toongabbee –
  At all those places I've worked in chains:
But of all the places of condemnation,
  In each penal station of New South Wales,
To Moreton Bay I found no equal,
  For excessive tyranny each day prevails.

Early in the morning when day is dawning,
  To trace from heaven the morning dew,
Up we are started at a moment's warning,
  Our daily labour to renew.
Our overseers and superintendents –
  These tyrants' orders we must obey,
Or else at the triangles our flesh is mangled –
  Such are our wages at Moreton Bay!

For three long years I've been beastly treated;
  Heavy irons each day I wore;
My back from flogging has been lacerated,
  And oftimes painted with crimson gore.
Like the Egyptians and ancient Hebrews,
  We were oppressed under Logan's yoke,
Till kind Providence came to our assistance,
  And gave this tyrant his mortal stroke.

Yes, he was hurried from that place of bondage,
  Where he thought he would gain renown;
But a native black, who lay in ambush,
  Gave this monster his fatal wound.

My fellow-prisoners, be exhilarated –
    That all such monsters such a death may find:
For it's when from bondage we are extricated,
    Our former sufferings will fade from mind.'

The Convict's Tour of Hell

Come all you prisoners of New South Wales,
Who frequent watch-houses and gaols;
A story unto you I'll tell,
About a convict's tour of hell.

This hero's valour had been tried,
Upon the highway before he died.
At length he fell to death a prey,
Which prov'd to him a happy day.
Downward he went, as I've been told,
Like one that's destined to Satan's fold,
Until he came to the River Styx,
When Charon's gaze was on him fixed.
'Friend!' said he, 'whence comest thou?
Thy name and business I must trow!'
'Well old Craft if you wish to know it
On earth they called me "Frank the Poet".'
'Oh well! fivepence or sixpence I daily charge
For a light passage in my barge,
But witty guest, I'd have you know it,
I never intend to charge a poet.'
So with a fair wind and flowing tide,
We wherry'd over to the other side,
Where leaving Charon at the ferry,
I journeyed on to Purgatory.

I boldly knocked at the gate,
Of Limbo, or the Middle State.
Pope Pius the seventh soon appeared,
With crown, cross, crucifix and beard.

'All hail!' cried Pius, 'but why this visit,
It's never Frank the Poet, is it?'
'Yes, and as for Heaven I am not fitted,
I hope in here to be admitted.'
Then said Pius, 'Vain are all your hopes,
For this is a place for priests and popes
And as its a crib of our own invention
We haven't got the least intention,
To admit such a foolish elf
Who scarce on earth could bless himself.'
'Oh well!' said I, 'I've no desire,
To enter this place of fire,
Where there's nothing but weeping, wailing and gnashing
And torments of the newest fashion,
And you must have been a foolish elf
To make a rod to beat yourself,
But may you and all your honest neighbours
Enjoy the fruits of all your labours!'
So bidding Pius a long farewell
I journeyed on to the place called Hell.

I knocked at the gate, then louder still,
When out rush'd the Devil, with, 'What's your will?'
'Oh!' said I, 'I've come here to dwell
And share my fate with you in hell.'
Cried Satan, 'That can't be I'm sure,
For I detest and hate the poor.
None shall in my kingdom stand
Except the wealthy and the grand.
So Frank! I think you've gone astray,
FOR CONVICTS NEVER COME THIS WAY,
But soar to heaven in droves and legions,
A place so called in the upper regions!'
'Oh well!' as I am in no hurry,
Have you got here one Capt. Murray?'
'Oh yes, he is within this place,
Would you like to see his face?'
'No, heaven forefend that I should view him,
For on board the *Phoenix* Hulk I knew him.

But who is that in yonder blaze
On fire and brimstone seems to graze?'
'He's Captain Logan, of Moreton Bay,
And Williams – killed the other day,
Was overseer at Grose's farm,
And did you convicts no small harm.
Cooke, who discovered New South Wales,
And he who first invented gaols,
Are both tied to a fiery stake
That stands in yonder boiling lake.
Hark! hear you not that dreadful yelling?
It comes from Dr Wardell's dwelling;
And yonder see those fiery chairs?
They're fitted up for Beaks and Mayors,
And men of all judicial orders,
Traps, bankers, lawyers and recorders.'

Then Frank saw legions of traitors,
Hangmen, gaolers, flagellators,
Commandants, constables, and spies;
Informers, overseers likewise,
In flames of brimstone they were toiling,
And lakes of sulphur round them boiling.
Hell resonant with hideous yelling;
Alas! how dismal was their dwelling.
Then Major Morrison he espied,
With Captain Clunie by his side.
They in fire-belt were lashed together
As tight as sole to upper leather;
Their situation here was horrid
For both were tyrants to the nor'ard.
Next he beheld old Sergeant Flood,
In Vulcan's hottest forge he stood;
He gazed on Frank – his eyes with ire
Appeared like burning coals of fire.
He by a red-hot clasping band
Was to a lofty lamp post chained:

With fiery garments all arrayed
Like wild Arabian ass he brayed.
Loud he implored for Frank's assistance
To end for him his sad existence.
'Cheer up,' said Frank, 'don't be dismayed,
Remember No. 3 Stockade;
In course of time you may do well
If you behave yourself in Hell.
Your heart on earth was fraught with malice,
You oft drove convicts to the gallows;
A greater rogue in shoes ne'er trod.
You now atone for all the blood
Of convicts shed by Sergeant Flood.'

He next beheld that noted trapman
And police-runner, Israel Chapman.
Steeped was he standing to his head
In cauldron hot of boiling lead.
'Alas!' he cried, 'behold me stranger,
I've captured many a bold bushranger,
For which I now am suffering here,
But lo! now yonder snakes appear.'
Then Frank beheld some loathly worms
And snakes of varied shapes and forms,
All entering at the mouth and ears
To gnaw his guts for endless years.
He next beheld the Co.'s Commissioner
At knee like humblest petitioner.
'Satan,' he cried, 'my life is ended;
For many years I've superintended
The Agricultural Co.'s affairs
And punctually paid all arrears.
But if you doubt the hopping colonel
At Carrington you'll find my journal
Careful writ out in black and white,
'T will prove that my accounts are right.'

The Poet turned to go away,
But Lucifer begged he would stay.
'Now Poet Frank, stay; don't you go man,
Till you see your old friend Dr Bowman;
See how he trembles, writhes and gnashes,
He gave *you* many a thousand lashes,
And for those same he does bewail;
While Oscar with his iron flail
Thrashes him well you may depend,
And will – till time shall have an end.'
Just as he spoke a coach and four
Came up in post haste to the door,
And some six feet of mortal sin,
Sans leave or licence tumbled in.
At its arrival cheers were given
That reached from Hell to Highest Heaven,
And all the denizens of Hell
With one rope pealed the greatest bell
That e'er was known to sound or ring
Since Judas sold our Heavenly King.
Drums were beating, flags were hoisting,
Never before was such rejoicing;
Dancing, singing, joy and mirth,
In Heaven above – and on the earth.
Straightway to Lucifer Frank went
To learn what these rejoicings meant.
'Of sense,' cried Satan, 'I'm deprived
Since Governor Darling has arrived;
Brimstone and fire I've ordered him,
And Vulcan has his tools in trim.
And I'll now find a fixed abode,
For Colonel Wilson's on the road.
Don't go, Frank, till you see the novice,
The Colonel from the Police Office.'
'Sir,' answered Frank, 'I'm satisfied
To learn that he is to be tied
And tortured in this world of fire:
With your leave, sir, I'll now retire.'

Then after travelling many days
O'er fiery hills and boiling seas,
At length he found that happy place
Where all the woes of mortal cease;
And rapping boldly at the wicket,
Says Peter, 'Show your certificate!
Or if you have got none to show
Pray, Who in Heaven do you know?'
'Why, sir! I know Jack Donohue,
And Johnny Troy, and Jenkins, too,
Whose backs by scourgings have been mangled
And at last by Jack Ketch were strangled.'

'Peter,' the Son said, 'Let Frank in,
For he is truly purged from sin;
Altho' in convict costume drest
Here shall he be a welcome guest!
Enoch! Go you with him to Job,
And put on him a silken robe.
Saint Paul! Go to the flock straightway,
And kill a calf or two today.
Tell Abraham, and likewise Abel,
In haste to lay the banquet table,
For we will make a grand repast,
Since Frank the Poet has come at last.'
Soon Moses came, likewise Elias,
John Baptist and his pal Mathias,
With many saints from foreign lands,
And with the Poet all shook hands.
Thro' Heaven's concave curfew rang,
And hymns of praise they loudly sang;
And while they glorified their theme,
I woke – and found it was a dream.

ANON

FIVE EARLY BUSHRANGING BALLADS

Jack Donahoe, transported from Dublin for 'intent to commit a felony', was easily the best-known of the convict 'bolters' who became bushrangers. After three years at large he was shot dead in a fight with the Horse Police in September 1830.

The Jim Jones, mentioned in the second song, does not seem to have been any particular real person but simply a type. The Johnny Troy of the third song seems, on the other hand, to have been an actual 'bolter' though he has not yet been identified. Even the ballad about him has survived in various versions, not in Australia but in the United States, as Professor Kenneth Porter of the University of Oregon first showed.

Martin Cash, transported from Ireland for housebreaking, was a Tasmanian bushranger who twice escaped from Port Arthur. In later years, after the transportation system had ended, Cash lived peaceably as a farmer near Hobart, enjoying the respect of his neighbours until his death in 1870.

Bold Jack Donahoe

In Dublin town I was brought up, in that city of great fame –
My decent friends and parents, they will tell to you the same.
It was for the sake of five hundred pounds I was sent across
    the main,
For seven long years in New South Wales to wear the convict's
    chain.

Chorus:

Then come, my hearties, we'll roam the mountains high!
Together we will plunder, together we will die!
We'll wander over the mountains and we'll gallop over plains –
For we scorn to live in slavery, bound down with iron chains.

I'd scarce been there twelve months or more upon the Aust-
ralian shore,
When I took to the highway, as I'd oft-times done before.
There was me and Jacky Underwood, Webber and Walmsley
too,
These were the true associates of bold Jack Donahoe.

Now Donahoe was taken, all for a notorious crime,
And sentenced to be hanged upon the gallows-tree so high.
But when they came to Sydney gaol he left them in a stew,
And when they came to call the roll they missed bold Donahoe.

As Donahoe made his escape, to the bush he went straightway.
The people they were all afraid to travel night and day —
For every week in the newspapers there was published some-
thing new
Concerning this dauntless hero, the bold Jack Donahoe!

As Donahoe was cruising, one summer's afternoon,
Little was his notion his death was near so soon,
When a sergeant of the horse police discharged his car-a-bine,
And called aloud on Donahoe to fight or to resign.

'Resign to you - you cowardly dogs! a thing I ne'er will do,
For I'll fight this night with all my might,' cried bold Jack
Donahoe.
'I'd rather roam these hills and dales, like wolf or kangaroo
Than work one hour for Government!' cried bold Jack
Donahoe.

He fought six rounds with the horse police until the fatal ball,
Which pierced his heart with cruel smart, caused Donahoe to
fall.
And as he closed his mournful eyes, he bade this world Adieu
Saying, 'Convicts all, pray for the soul of Bold Jack Donahoe!'

Jack Donahoe and His Gang

A life that is free as the bandits' of old,
When Rome was the prey of the warriors bold,
Who knew how to buy gallant soldiers with gold,
  Is the life full of danger
  Of Jack, the bushranger,
  Of brave Donahoe!

If Ireland lies groaning, a hand at her throat,
Which foreigners have from the recreants bought,
Forget not the lessons our fathers have taught.
  Though our Isle's full of danger,
  And held by the stranger,
  Be brave and be true!

I've left the old Island's hospitable shores,
The land of the Emmets, the Tones, and the Moores;
But Liberty o'er me her scalding tear pours,
  And she points to the manger,
  Where *He* was a stranger,
  And perished for you.

Then hurl me to crime and brand me with shame,
But think not to baulk me, my spirit to tame,
For I'll fight to the last in old Ireland's name.
  Though I be a bushranger,
  You still are the stranger,
  And I'm Donahoe!

Jim Jones at Botany Bay

O, listen for a moment lads, and hear me tell my tale –
How, o'er the sea from England's shore I was compelled to sail.

The jury says 'he's guilty, sir,' and says the judge, says he –
'For life, Jim Jones, I'm sending you across the stormy sea;

And take my tip, before you ship to join the Iron-gang,
Don't be too gay at Botany Bay, or else you'll surely hang –

Or else you'll surely hang,' says he – 'and after that, Jim Jones,
High up upon th' gallow-tree the crows will pick your bones.

You'll have no chance for mischief then; remember what I say,
They'll flog th' poachin' out of you, out there at Botany Bay!'

The winds blew high upon th' sea, and th' pirates came along,
But the soldiers on our convict ship were full five hundred
   strong.

They opened fire and somehow drove that pirate ship away.
I'd have rather joined that pirate ship than have come to
   Botany Bay:

For night and day the iron clang, and like poor galley slaves
We toil, and toil, and when we die must fill dishonoured
   graves.

But bye-and-bye I'll break my chains: into the bush I'll go,
And join the brave bushrangers – Jack Donohoe and Co.;

And some dark night when everything is silent in the town
I'll kill the tyrants, one and all; and shoot th' floggers down:

I'll give th' law a little shock: remember what I say,
They'll yet regret they sent Jim Jones in chains to Botany Bay!

Johnny Troy

Come all ye daring bushrangers and outlaws of the land,
Who scorn to live in slavery or wear the convict's band.
I'll tell to you the story of the most heroic boy:
All the country knew him by the name of Johnny Troy.

Troy was born in Dublin, that city of great fame,
Brought up by honest parents; the world knows the same.
From the robbing of a widow, he was sent o'er the main,
For Seven Years in New South Wales to wear a convict's
    chain.

There were a hundred and forty serving out their times,
Some of them for murder, and some for smaller crimes.
Johnny Troy was one among them and solemnly he swore:
'This very night I'll free you all, or I shall be no more.'

There were six well-armed policemen all seated in the bow;
And they were none much surprised when Johnny com-
    menced his row.
And they were none of them much surprised when Troy he
    made a rush;
And six more as brave heroes plunged bravely in the bush.

'And it's now we've gained our liberty, our escape we will
    make sure;
We'll smash and break those handcuffs when once we reach
    the shore.
'When once we reach the shore, brave boys, we'll shout and
    sing for joy;
We'll hiss and stone those horse-police and sing "Bold
    Johnny Troy."'

There were Troy, Bill Harrington, Tim Jackson, and Jack
    Dunn,
Four of the bravest heroes who ever handled gun.
They chanced to meet an old man all on the king's highway,
And Troy rode up to him while these words he did say,

'Your gold watch and your money I quickly do demand,
Or I'll blow out your brains instantly, if you refuse to stand.'
'I've neither watch nor money,' the old man then replied;
'But for a wife and family I daily do provide.

'I've been cast out of the Shamrock Isle for being a reckless
    boy.'
'But if that's so, you shan't be robbed,' cried gallant Johnny
    Troy.
Troy then mounted on his steed, and before he rode away,
He said, 'Here's fifty pounds, old man, 'twill help you on
    your way.

'The poor I'll serve both night and day, the rich I will annoy;
The people round know me right well; they call me "Johnny
    Troy."'
Said Troy to Bill Harrington, 'Load every man his piece;
For this very night I intend to fight against the horse-police.'

Now Johnny Troy was captured and sentenced then to die
Upon the tenth of April upon the scaffold high.
His friends and all that knew him, wept for this fearless boy:
'There goes our brave young hero by the name of Johnny
    Troy!'

Martin Cash, the Gentleman Bushranger

Come all you sons of Erin's Isle that love to hear your tuneful
    notes –
Rember William Wallace and Montrose of Sweet Dundee –
Napoleon played his part: by treachery undone –
The great Nelson, for England's glory, bled and nobly fought
    by sea –
And Wellington, old Erin's son, who Waterloo so bravely won
When leading on his veteran troops, bold faced his daring foes:
None of these warriors could compare with our dauntless
    gentleman bushranger,
Bold Martin Cash of matchless fame, where the sprig of sham-
    rock grows.

By treachery, as it is said, this hero to a gaol was led:
'Twas Bedford who, in Campbell Town, had got him seven
    years,
Which sent him to the settlement in misery and discontent,
But soon he made his foes repent, as you shall quickly hear.
He left Port Arthur's cursed soil, saying 'No longer will I toil,'
And soon he reached the Derwent's side in spite of all his foes.
He made the settlers crouch in dread, where e'er he showed
    his head –
This valiant son of Erin, where the sprig of shamrock grows.

It was once when near the Woolpack Inn by enemies attacked:
The number being three to one, they thought their prize secure:
But Martin to his piece did cling, and three of them did quickly
    wing,
Saying, 'Down! you cowardly dogs, or I will nail you to the
    floor.'
It's loud for mercy they did cry, but no one came to their reply,
While Martin with a smiling eye, stood gazing at his foes.
Then through the bush he made his way, and called on settlers
    night and day,
Did our valiant son of Erin, where the sprig of shamrock grows.

It was on the Salt Pan Plains he faced his enemies again,
There were Sydney blacks and horse-police and well-trained
    soldiers too;
But at the time when they drew near, Cash hailed them loudly
    with a cheer,
And let them have it left and right, his colours were true blue –
Bravely did he stand his ground, the bullets flying thick around,
And like a fearless general he faced his firing foes.
'Surrender Martin,' loud they cry, 'Never till the hour I die'
Said this valiant son of Erin, where the sprig of shamrock
    grows.

Brave Cash not caring for his life, to Hobart came to see his
    wife.
The constables who lay in wait cried, 'Martin is in view.'

Some cowards tried to block his way but one of them soon
    lifeless lay:
Their numbers were increasing and still Cash did pursue,
And in the street a man rushed out, who tried to stop him in
    his route,
But with a pistol in each hand he shot clean off his nose.
'Surrender Cash!' was still their cry, 'Never till the hour I die,'
Said this gallant son of Erin, where the sprig of shamrock
    grows.

O'er-powered and wounded, bleeding, pale, the Bobbies
    walked him off to gaol,
And when his trial was brought on, some hundreds listened by:
And when the judge with panting breath had told him to
    prepare for death,
He calmly heard the sentence with a proud unflinching eye.
We all have hopes that we shall see brave Martin yet at liberty,
That shortly he will be as free as the ocean wind that blows.
He's of a good old valiant race, there's no one can his name
    disgrace,
He's a noble son of Erin, where the sprig of shamrock grows.

He's the bravest man that you could choose from Sydney men
    or Cockatoos
And a gallant son of Erin, where the sprig of shamrock grows.

ANON

These verses probably began as a song written for the popular stage in the Sydney of the 1840s. They reflect not only the new chum's bewilderment but also the degree to which most of the audience had already made themselves at home in the new environment.

Paddy Malone

Oh my name's Pat Malone 'twas in sweet Tipperary,
I don't know what 'tis now, I'm so bothered ochone,
The girls that I've danced with light hearted and airy,
Would hardly remember poor Paddy Malone.
It's twelve months or so since our ship she cast anchor
In happy Australia the immigrants' home,
From that day to this there's been trouble and canker,
And grief and vexation for Paddy Malone.
Musha, Paddy Malone; Arrah, Paddy Malone,
'Twas a thief of an agent that coaxed you from home.

With a man called a Squatter I soon got a place sure,
He'd a beard like a goat, and such whiskers, ochone,
And he said as he looked thro' the hair on his face sure,
That he *liked* the appearance of Paddy Malone.
So he hired me at once to go up to his station,
Saying abroad in the bush, you'll find yourself at home.
Faith, I *liked* the proposal, so without hesitation,
Signed my name with a X *crass* that spells Paddy Malone
Musha, Paddy Malone, you're no writer Marrone,
But you can leave your mark my brave Paddy Malone.

So I herded the sheep in the bush as he called it,
'Twas no bush at all, but a mighty big wood,
With old ancient trees that were small bushes one time,
A long time ago I suppose 'fore the flood.
So to find out this big bush one day I went farther,
The trees grew so thick I couldn't find it, ochone,
I turned to come back, but that was much harder

So bothered and lost was poor Paddy Malone.
Poor Paddy Malone thro' the wild bush did roam,
What a babe in the wood was poor Paddy Malone.

I was soon overcome then with grief and vexation,
So I camped you must know by the side of a log,
I was found the next day, by a man from the station,
I coo-eed and roared like a bull in a bog,
Says the master that day to me, Pat where's the sheep now,
Faith says I, I don't know, I see one here at home.
Sure he took the hint and kicked up a big row,
And said, he'd stop the wages of Paddy Malone.
Now Paddy Malone, you're no shepherd you'll own,
So we'll try you at bullocks, brave Paddy Malone.

Oh to see me dressed out with my team and my dray too,
My whip like a flail and such gaiters you'd own,
The bullocks as they eye's me, the brutes seemed to say now,
Do your best Paddy, we're blessed if we'll go.
Gee Redman says I, Come hither Damper,
Whoop Blackbird and Magpie, Gee up there Wallone,
The brutes they turned short and away they did scamper,
And head over heels they pitched Paddy Malone.
Oh Paddy Malone, sure you've seen Bulls at home,
But the Bulls of Australia, Cow Paddy Malone.

I was found the next day where bullocks had threw me,
By a man passing by, upon hearing me groan.
After wiping the mud from my face then he knew me,
Why, says he, your name's Paddy, yes Paddy Malone.
Oh! murder says I, you're an Angel sent down sure,
Says he no I'm not, but a friend of your own,
So with his persuasion I started for town sure,
And you see now before you poor Paddy Malone.
Arrah, Paddy Malone, you've been cheated Malone,
Bad luck to that agent that coaxed you from home!

ANON

This is possibly the most popular of all Australian folk-songs dating from the first half of the last century. It is still remembered, in innumerable versions, by many old singers.

The marriage *motif* is, as appears plainly in the last stanza, lightly satirical. In the 1840s in the Squatting districts the ratio of unmarried males over fourteen years of age to unmarried females (ditto) was about forty to one, and even in Sydney the ratio was about two to one. An Aboriginal woman was the only kind of 'wife' most bush-workers of the period could realistically hope for.

The Old Bullock Dray

Oh! the shearing is all over, and the wool is coming down,
And I mean to get a wife, boys, when I go down to town.
Everything that's got two legs presents itself to view,
From the little paddy-melon to the bucking kangaroo.

Chorus:
So it's roll up your blankets, and let's make a push,
I'll take you up the country and show you the bush.
I'll be bound you won't get such a chance another day,
So come and take possession of my old Bullock-dray.

Now, I've saved up a good cheque and I mean to buy a team,
And when I get a wife, boys, I'll be all-serene;
For, calling at the depot, they say there's no delay
To get an off-sider for the old Bullock-dray.

I'll teach you the whip, and the bullocks how to flog,
You'll be my off-sider when we're stuck in a bog:
Lashing out both left and right and every other way,
Making skin, hair and blood fly round the old Bullock-dray.

Oh! we'll live like fighting-cocks, for good living I'm your
    man.
We'll have leather-jacks, johnny-cakes, and fritters in the
    pan;
Or if you want some fish, why, I'll catch you some soon;
For we'll bob for barramundies round the banks of a
    lagoon.

Oh! yes, of beef and damper I make sure we have enough,
And we'll boil in the bucket such a whopper of a duff;
And our friends will dance to the honour of the day,
To the music of the bells, around the old Bullock-dray.

Oh! we'll have plenty girls, we must mind that.
There'll be 'Buck-jumping Maggie' and 'Leather-belly Pat.'
There'll be 'Stringbark Peggy' and 'Green-Hide Mike,'
Yes, my Colonials, just as many as you like!

Now we'll stop all immigration, we don't need it any more;
We'll be having young natives, twins by the score.
And I wonder what the devil Jack Robertson would say
If he saw us promenading round the old Bullock-dray.

Oh! it's time I had an answer, if there's one to be had,
I wouldn't treat that steer in the body half as bad;
But he takes as much notice of me, upon my soul,
As that old blue stag off-sider in the pole.

Oh! to tell a lot of lies, you know, it is a sin,
But I'll go up the country and marry a black gin.
'Baal gammon white feller,' that is what she'll say,
'Budgery you and your old Bullock-dray!'

ANON

These verses from a Melbourne paper of 1856 give a somewhat romanticised picture of the 'old Australian squatter' of the preceding 'pastoral age' (about 1830 to 1851), during which the best parts of the interior were first occupied by graziers.

The Squatter of the Olden Time

I'll sing to you a fine new song, made by my blessed mate,
Of a fine Australian squatter who had a fine estate,
Who swore by right pre-emptive at a sanguinary rate
That by his rams, his ewes, his lambs, Australia was made great –
    Like a fine Australian squatter, one of the olden time.

His hut around was hung with guns, whips, spurs and boots, and shoes,
And kettles and tin pannikins to hold the tea he brews;
And here his worship lolls at ease and takes his smoke and snooze,
And quaffs his cup of hysonskin, the beverage old chums choose –
    Like a fine Australian squatter, one of the olden time.

And when shearing-time approaches he opens hut to all,
And though ten thousand are his flocks, he quickly shears them all,
Even to the scabby wanderer you'd think no good at all;
For while he fattens all the great, he boils down all the small –
    Like a fine old Murray squatter, one of the olden time.

And when his worship comes to town his agents for to see,
His wool to ship, his beasts to sell, he lives right merrily;
The club his place of residence, as becomes a bush J.P.,
He darkly hints that Thompson's run from scab is scarcely free –
    This fine old Murray settler, one of the olden time.

And now his fortune he has make to England straight goes he,
But finds with grief he's not received as he had hoped to be.
His friends declare his habits queer, his language much too free,
And are somewhat apt to cross the street when him they
chance to see –
This fine old Australian squatter, the boy of the olden time.

II

(1851-61)

THE GOLD RUSH: NEW CHUMS AND DIGGERS

_____

JUST as bullock-drivers, squatters, and others were beginning to feel at home in Australia, rich gold-fields were discovered in 1851. Within ten years the population of the continent had increased nearly three-fold. For a time it seemed that the tidal-wave of new chums would swamp the characteristically Australian manners and attitudes which had begun to develop. In the long run, however it was the newcomers who changed to take on the colour of their surroundings.

The following songs illustrate the process.

CHARLES THATCHER (1831-78)

A witty and reasonably well-educated Englishman, the twenty-one year old Thatcher reached Melbourne in November 1852. He left at once for the gold-fields, but soon discovered he could make more money by singing to the diggers than by digging for gold himself. At Ballarat and Bendigo, the main Victorian gold towns, he composed hundreds of topical songs about gold-fields' life and Australian ways. He became known as 'the inimitable Thatcher', or simply 'the inimitable', as his reputation as a stage-singer and entertainer grew. The next five ballads are fair samples of his work. Some of them, like _The Queer Ways of Australia_, were so popular that they were passed on by word of mouth and changed in the process until their true origin was forgotten and they were accepted, properly enough, as genuine folk-songs.

The only considerably bloody riot, or pitched battle, ever fought on Australian soil occurred on the Eureka Lead at Ballarat on 3 December 1854, when a rebellion of gold-diggers was

defeated by soldiers and policemen. Thatcher's *Licence-Hunting*
describes the provocative police practices which did a good deal
to cause the revolt. *Captain Bumble's Letter* jeers satirically at
the victorious, but unpopular, soldiers.

The New-Chum Swell

I'll sing just now a little song,
For you must understand,
'Tis of a fine young gentleman,
That left his native land –
That bid his ma and pa farewell,
And started brave and bold,
In a ship of fourteen hundred tons,
To come and dig for gold.

His dress was spicy as could be,
His fingers hung with rings,
White waistcoats, black silk pantaloons,
And other stylish things.
His berth was in the cuddy,
Which is on deck, you know,
And all the intermediates
He voted 'deuced low.'

When the vessel left the London Docks,
Most jovial did he seem;
But in the Downs, a change came o'er
The spirit of his dream.
His ruddy cheeks turned very pale,
His countenance looked rum,
And with a mournful sigh, said he,
'I wish I'd never come.'

The ship at length cast anchor,
And he was glad once more;
Six large trunks he then packed up,
And started for the shore –

His traps quite filled a whale-boat,
So of course I needn't say,
That for the freight thereof, he had
A tidy sum to pay.

He came to town, and then put up
At the Criterion Hotel
If you've been there, you know the place,
And the charges pretty well.
He played at billiards half the day,
And smoked and lounged about,
Until the hundred pounds he'd brought,
Had precious near run out.

With five pounds in his pocket,
He went to Bendigo;
And when he saw the diggings,
They filled his heart with woe –
'What! must I venture down a hole,
And throw up filthy clay?
If my mother could but see me now,
Whatever would she say?'

He went and bought a shovel
And a pick and dish as well;
But to every ten minutes' work,
He took an hour's spell.
The skin from off his fair, white hands
In blisters peeled away –
And thus he worked, and sunk about
Twelve inches every day.

When off the bottom just a foot,
He got quite out of heart,
And threw his pick down in a rage,
And off he did depart;
But when he'd left his hole, and gone,
A cove named Sydney Bob

Stepped into it, and soon took out
A pretty handsome 'lob'.

With five shillings in his pocket,
He started in disgust,
And then he went upon the roads
As many a young swell must:
And if through the Black Forest
You ever chance to stray,
You may see him do the Gov'ment stroke
At eight bob every day.

Gold-fields Girls

What a rum lot the girls are out here:
    They jolly soon get colonized, sirs,
I twig their rum capers sometimes,
    And feel not a little surprised, sirs.
As regards love and marriage out here,
    I'm fairly licked clean off my perch, sirs;
One day they pick up a chap,
    The next day he's walked off to church, sirs.

If at home you should flirt with a girl,
    In a twinkling the old bloke, her father,
Asks what your intentions may be,
    And isn't he down on you rather!
The mother leads you in a string,
    And sticks to you like bricks and mortar,
For she's always talking to you
    About her accomplished daughter.

The courtship lasts some little time,
    And then of course you pop the question,
She immediately bursts into tears,
    And calls it a cruel suggestion;

She falters out 'ask my papa,'
　　When you beg her to be your dear wife, sirs,
And in two or three weeks from that time,
　　You find that you're tied up for life, sirs.

But things are far different here:
　　The girls don't consult their relations.
What's father or mother to them?
　　They follow their own inclinations.
If you name the day here to a gal,
　　Don't think off her perch it will lick her,
For nine out of ten will reply
　　'*Lor, Sammy, can't it be done quicker?*'

The best of this colony is,
　　The brides have no fine affectation:
In saying 'I will' they're 'all there',
　　And they don't faint upon the occasion.
A bottle lots of 'em will use,
　　And it seems to come in very handy,
You might think that it's Preston salts,
　　No fear! the smell tells you it's brandy.

The bride's mother, too, will be there,
　　She's not overcome by emotion,
Her spirits you find she keeps up
　　By Old Tom or some other lotion;
And sometimes her voice will grow thick.
　　In her speech there's a wond'rous obstruction,
But her friends are to blame for it all;
　　For they ought to allowance her suction.

But some brides upon their wedding night,
　　In colonial parlance get '*tight*', sirs,
And then in that state they evince
　　A strong inclination to fight, sirs.
They've been known to take tumblers up
　　And shy them in every direction,
But bless their dear hearts, we all know
　　It's proof of colonial affection!

Licence-Hunting

The morning was fine,
The sun brightly did shine;
   The diggers were working away –
When the inspector of traps
Said, 'now my fine chaps,
   We'll go licence hunting today.'
Some went this way; some that,
Some to Bendigo Flat;
   And a lot to the White Hills did tramp –
Whilst a lot more did bear,
Towards Golden Square;
   And the rest of them kept round the camp.

Each turned his eye
To the holes he went by –
   Expecting down on them to drop;
But not one could they nail,
For they'd given leg bail,
   Diggers ain't often caught on the hop.
The little word 'Joe',
Which all of you know,
   Is a signal that the traps are quite near;
Made them all cut their sticks,
And they hooked it like bricks;
   'I believe you, my boy – no fear.'

Now a tall ugly trap,
Espied a young chap,
   Up the gully cutting like fun;
So he quickly gave chase,
But 'twas a hard race –
   I assure you the digger could run.
Down a hole he went pop,
Whilst the bobby up top,
   Says, 'just come up,' shaking his staff:

'Young man of the crown,
If you want me come down;
    For I'm not to be caught with such chaff.'

Now, some would have thought,
The sly fox he'd have caught,
    By lugging him out of the hole;
But this cruster, no fear,
Quite scorned the idea
    Of going underground like a mole.
But wiser by half,
He put by his staff,
    And as onward he went said he –
'When a cove's down a "drive",
Whether dead or alive,
    He may stay there till Christmas for me!'

Captain Bumble's Letter

Don't talk about Sebastopol,
    The Russian War is flat now.
Just listen to despatches
    Just come from Ballarat now.
Our noble Governor, Sir Charles,
    And where is there a better,
Has permitted us to publish
    Captain Bumble's private letter.

He writes thus to His Excellency,
    'Myself and Major Stiggins
Got our brave fellows all equipped
    And started for the diggins.
Our band struck up God Save the Queen,
    Into cheers our men were bursting,
And every gallant soldier was
    For glorious action thirsting.

'Our first attack was on two drays
    Which we saw in the distance,
But the enemy surrendered
    After just a slight resistance.
We were disappointed in our search
    Of these two wretched traitors,
For instead of siezing powder
    It was loaded with potatoes.

'We marched but were obliged to halt
    On behalf of Sergeant Trunnions,
Who was unable to proceed
    On account of having bunions.
We stationed pickets all around
    To give us timely warning
And there we bivouacked and slept
    Till nine the following morning.

'At length into the diggins,
    Footsore our men did tramp there,
And we took up our position
    Within the Gov'ment camp there:
Provisions were served out to all
    And my very soul it tickles
To contemplate their ravages
    On the cold boiled beef and pickles.

'We watched at night, but all was still:
    For glory we were yearning,
And we fired upon a tent in which
    A candle was seen burning.
We killed a woman and a child
    Though 'twas not our intention;
But that slight mistakes occur
    Of course I needn't mention.

'At length in earnest was the strife:
    While buried in their slumbers,
We made a bold and desperate charge
    And cut them down in numbers.

Our gallant fellows fought like bricks
   The rebels were defeated,
And then by hundreds off they ran
   And to the bush retreated.

'Thus all is quiet and I now
   Subscribe myself your humble
Devoted servant of the Crown,
   Frederick Augustus Bumble.

Postscript
Pray send us up some good cheroots
   And anything that's handy
And by all means, pray don't forget
   We're nearly out of brandy.'

The Queer Ways of Australia

Dick Briggs, a wealthy farmer's son,
To England lately took a run,
To see his friends, and have some fun,
For he'd been ten years in Australia.
Arrived in England, off he went
To his native village down in Kent –
'Twas there his father drew his rent,
And many happy days he'd spent.
No splendid, fine clothes on had he,
But jumper'n boots up to the knee,
With dirty Sydney 'cabbage-tree' –
The costume of Australia.

Chorus:
Now when a fellow takes a run
To England for a bit of fun,
He's sure to 'stonish everyone
With the queer ways of Australia.

Now Dick went home in this array;
His sister came out and did say,
'No, we don't want anything today,'
To her brother from Australia.
Cried he, 'Oh, don't you know poor Dick?'
They recognized him precious quick;
The 'old man' hugged him like a brick.
And there was feasting there that night,
For Richard was a welcome sight,
For each one hailed with great delight
The wanderer from Australia.

The blessed cattle on the farm
Regarded Dick with great alarm;
His swearing acted like a charm
When he gave them a 'touch' of Australia.
He could talk 'bullock' and 'no flies',
And when he blessed poor Strawberry's eyes,
She looked at him with great surprise
As out of her he 'took a rise'.
'Fie, fie,' his mother said one day,
'What naughty, wicked words you say.'
'Bless you, mother, that's the way
We wake 'em up in Australia.'

Dick went to London for a spree,
And got drunk there most gloriously;
He gave them a touch of 'Coo-oo-ee'
The bush cry of Australia.
He took two ladies to the play,
Both so serene, in dresses gay,
He had champagne brought on a tray
And said, 'Now girls, come fire away.'
They drank till they could drink no more,
And then they both fell on the floor.
Cried Dick, as he surveyed them o'er,
'You wouldn't do for Australia!'

This gold-fields folk-song developed in oral tradition from an older song, *Like a True-born Irishman*. 'Lighthouse' in the last stanza is a joking synonym for 'swag', the usually cylindrical bundle of blankets and other belongings which gold-diggers and bushmen carried strapped to their backs when tramping from one locality to another.

Like a True-born Native Man

When first I left Old England's shore
　Such yarns as we were told,
As how folks in Australia
　Could pick up lumps of gold.
So, when we got to Melbourne Town,
　We were ready soon to slip
And get even with the captain –
　All hands scuttled from the ship.

Chorus
With my swag all on my shoulder,
　Black billy in my hand,
I travelled the bush of Australia
　Like a true-born native man.

We steered our course for Geelong Town,
　Then north-west to Ballarat,
Where some of us got mighty thin,
　And some got sleek and fat.
Some tried their luck at Bendigo,
　And some at Fiery Creek;
I made a fortune in a day
　And spent it in a week.

For many years I wandered round,
　As each new rush broke out,
And always had of gold a pound,
　Till alluvial petered out.

'Twas then we took the bush to cruise,
　　Glad to get a bite to eat;
The squatters treated us so well
　　We made a regular beat.

So round the 'lighthouse' now I tramp
　　Nor leave it out of sight;
I take it on my left shoulder,
　　And then upon my right,
And then I take it on my back,
　　And oft upon it lie.
It is the best of tucker tracks
　　So I'll stay here till I die.

III

(1861-85)

SETTLING DOWN: EARLY TRADITIONAL BUSH BALLADS

As the gold-fever began to die down, it became clear that the pattern of up-country life had not changed so very much. Many new-chum diggers went to swell the population of the growing colonial capitals but some, like those addressed in *Stringy-bark and Green-hide*, stayed in the bush and thus became completely 'colonized' the more quickly.

Bushrangers continued – at least in the view of their numerous admirers – to rob the rich and help the poor. In this period few of them were ex-convicts with a grudge against society. Most were native-born lads, inspired by love of show and adventure, as well as by the deep convict-derived tradition of hostility to the police and constituted authority generally. When they killed people who were not policemen, they usually forfeited all popular sympathy. Thus Ben Hall, the Kelly Gang, the anonymous 'Wild Colonial Boy' who may or may not have derived from Bold Jack Donahoe, are still praised as heroes in folk song and story: but Wilson, who murdered 'Gallant Peter Clark' is execrated.

Shearers and other itinerant bush-workers continued to 'lamb down' or squander their cheques in drunken sprees, between bouts of hard work: partly because, as *They've All Got a Mate but Me* implies, there were still so few women in the bush that most men had little incentive to save for marriage. John Robertson and other thoughtful politicians tried to remedy the situation by passing free-selection acts, which sought to establish a class of self-employed small farmers in the bush. However, until government railways provided cheap transport for wheat in the last decade or two of the nineteenth century, many farmers or 'cockies' had to choose between cattle-duffing described in *The Eumerella Shore* or the grinding poverty which was too often the lot of the hard-working and honest selector such as *The Cocky Farmer*.

Dating from 1866, this is another popular stage song which seems to have passed into oral tradition. Australians like to believe that they are particularly adept at improvisation, at 'making-do' with whatever rough-and-ready materials happen to be handy. By the 1840s a traditional saying had already grown up that 'if it were not for stringy-bark and green-hide the whole colony would go to hell.'

Stringy-bark and Green-hide

I sing of a commodity, it's one that will not fail yer,
I mean that common oddity, the mainstay of Australia;
Gold it is a precious thing, for commerce it increases,
But stringy-bark and green-hide, can beat it all to pieces.

Chorus:
Stringy-bark and green-hide, they will never fail yer!
Stringy-bark and green-hide are the mainstay of Australia!

If you travel on the road, and chance to stick in Bargo,
To avoid a bad capsize, you must unload your cargo;
For to pull your dray about, I do not see the force on,
Take a bit of green-hide, and hook another horse on.

If you chance to take a dray, and break your leader's traces,
Get a bit of green-hide, to mend your broken places;
Green-hide is a useful thing, all that you require,
But stringy-bark's another thing when you want a fire.

If you want to build a hut, to keep out wind and weather,
Stringy-bark will make it snug, and keep it well together;
Green-hide if it's used by you, will make it all the stronger,
For if you tie it with green-hide, it's sure to last the longer.

New chums to this golden land, never dream of failure,
Whilst you've got such useful things as these in fair Aus-
   tralia.
For stringy-bark and green-hide will never, never fail yer,
Stringy-bark and green-hide are the mainstay of Australia.

ANON

Native-born son of emancipist parents, Ben Hall was the most celebrated of all bushrangers until his fame was later eclipsed by that of Ned Kelly. Under circumstances not very different from those detailed in this ballad, he was killed near Forbes by a large detachment of policemen in 1865.

Brave Ben Hall

Come all Australian sons with me
   For a hero has been slain,
And cowardly butchered in his sleep
   Upon the Lachlan Plain.

Pray do not stay your seemly grief,
   But let a tear-drop fall;
For manly hearts will always mourn
   The fate of Bold Ben Hall.

No brand of Cain e'er stamped his brow,
   No widow's curse did fall;
When tales are read, the squatters dread
   The name of Bold Ben Hall.

The records of this hero bold
   Through Europe have been heard,
And formed the conversation
   Between many an Earl and Lord.

Ever since the good old days
   Of Dick Turpin and Duval,
Knights of the road were outlaws bold,
   And so was Bold Ben Hall.

He never robbed a needy man –
   His records best will show –
Staunch and loyal to his mates,
   And manly to the foe.

Until he left his trusty mates –
   The cause I ne'er could hear –
The bloodhounds of the law heard this,
   And after him did steer.

They found his place of ambush,
   And cautiously they crept,
And savagely they murdered him
   Whilst their victim slept.

Yes, savagely they murdered him,
   Those cowardly blue-coat imps,
Who were laid on to where he slept,
   By informing peeler's pimps.

No more he'll mount his gallant steed,
   Nor range the mountains high.
The widow's friend in poverty,
   Bold Ben Hall! Good-bye!

The Wild Colonial Boy

There was a wild colonial boy, Jack Donahoe by name,
Of poor but honest parents he was born in Castlemaine.
He was his father's dearest hope, his mother's pride and joy.
O, fondly did his parents love their Wild Colonial Boy.

Chorus:
   So ride with me, my hearties, we'll cross the mountains high.
   Together we will plunder, together we will die.
   We'll wander through the valleys and gallop o'er the plains,
   For we scorn to live in slavery, bound down with iron chains!

He was scarcely sixteen years of age when he left his father's
   home,
A convict to Australia, across the seas to roam.

They put him in the Iron Gang in the Government employ,
But ne'er an iron on earth could hold the Wild Colonial Boy.

And when they sentenced him to hang to end his wild career,
With a loud shout of defiance bold Donahoe broke clear.
He robbed those wealthy squatters, their stock he did destroy,
But never a trap in the land could catch the Wild Colonial Boy.

Then one day when he was cruising near the broad Nepean's
   side,
From out the thick Bringelly bush the horse police did ride.
'Die or resign, Jack Donahoe!' they shouted in their joy.
'I'll fight this night with all my might!' cried the Wild Colonial
   Boy.

He fought six rounds with the horse police before the fatal ball,
Which pierced his heart with cruel smart, caused Donahoe to
   fall.
And then he closed his mournful eyes, his pistol an empty toy,
Crying: 'Parents dear, O say a prayer for the Wild Colonial
   Boy.'

Gallant Peter Clark

On Waldron's Range at morning light
   The sun shone brightly down:
It glittered on the winding Page
   Near Murrurundi town.

There stands a simple block of stone,
   Erected as a mark
To show the spot where he fought and died,
   The Gallant Peter Clark.

And if you will but listen awhile,
   To you I will relate
What happened there to Peter Clark
   And Jimmy Clark his mate.

They camped one night close by the Range:
  In songs the hours soon passed,
And little did poor Peter think
  That night would be his last.

At dawn they climbed the steep ascent,
  And scarce had reached the top,
When a voice in accents stern and loud
  Commanded them to stop.

'Hand over your money, watch and chain,'
  The robber boldly cried.
'Who takes my money takes my life,'
  The angry Clark replied.

Then laughed the robber loud in scorn,
  As he his pistol drew.
Said he, 'My hand is firm and strong:
  My aim is ever true.

'So give up your money now my lad,
  And do not idly rave:
Resist, and by the God above,
  This night you'll fill the grave.'

'Those are but words, and idle words,'
  The angry Clark replied;
And with one rapid bound he strode
  Close by the robber's side.

And now began the struggle
  For life between them both:
One hand of Clark's the pistol grasped,
  The other grasped his throat.

Now haste, now haste you, Jimmy Clark,
  Your mate is now in need.
Your comrade's welfare and his life
  Depend upon your speed!

Hark to that loud pistol-shot
   Whose echo rends the skies.
A human body on the sod
   In its death-struggle lies!

The robber, frightened by his deed,
   Terror-struck did stand;
When he felt a grip upon his arm –
   It was Jimmy's heavy hand.

'So now my lad I swear by Heaven
   That I shall see you die,
Not like a man, but like a dog,
   Upon the gallows high.'

And so indeed was Clark revenged,
   For God has said it so:
Who takes a life must yield a life,
   And murder met its due.

Ballad of Jack Lefroy

Come all you lads and listen, a story I would tell,
Before they take me out and hang me high;
My name is Jack Lefroy, and life I would enjoy,
But the old judge has sentenced me to die.
My mother she was Irish and she taught me at her knee,
But to steady work I never did incline,
As a youngster I could ride any horse was wrapped in hide,
And when I saw a good 'un he was mine.

Chorus:
So all young lads take warning and don't be led astray,
For the past you never, never can recall;
While young your gifts employ, take a lesson from Lefroy,
Let fate be a warning to you all.

Go straight, young man, they told me when my first long
    stretch was done;
If you're jugg'd again you'll have yourself to thank;
But I swore I'd not be found hunting nuggets in the ground
When the biggest could be picked up in the bank.
Well, I've stuck up some mail coaches, and I've ridden with
    Ben Hall,
And they never got me cornered once until
A pimp was in their pay – gave my dingo hole away,
And they run me to earth at Riley's Hill.

'Come out, Lefroy!' they called me: 'Come out, we're five to
    one;'
But I took my pistols out and stood my ground.
For an hour I pumped out lead till they got me in the head,
And when I awoke they had me bound.
It's a pleasant day to live, boys, a gloomy one to die,
A dangling with your neck inside a string,
How I'd like to ride again down the hills to Lachlan Plain!
But when the sun rises I must swing.

The Old Keg of Rum

My name is old Jack Palmer and I once dug for gold,
And the song I'm going to sing you recalls the days of old,
When I'd plenty mates around me and the talk would fairly
    hum
As we all sat together round the old keg of rum.

Chorus: The old keg of rum! the old keg of rum!
        As we all sat together round the old keg of rum!

There was Bluey Watt, the breaker, and old Tom Hines,
And Jimmy Doyle, the ringer, who now in Glory shines,
And many more hard doers, all gone to Kingdom Come,
We were all associated round the old keg of rum.

Chorus: The old keg of rum! the old keg of rum!
    We were all associated round the old keg of rum!

When shearing time was over at the sheds on the Bree,
We'd raise a keg from somewhere and we'd all have a spree.
We'd sit and sing together till we got that blind and dumb,
We couldn't find the bunghole of the old keg of rum.

Chorus: The old keg of rum! the old keg of rum!
     We couldn't find the bunghole of the old keg of rum!

There was some would last the night out and some have a
  snooze,
And some were full of fight, boys, and all were full of booze,
Till often in the scrimmage, I've corked it with my thumb
To keep the life from leaking from the old keg of rum!

Chorus: The old keg of rum! the old keg of rum!
     To keep the life from leaking from the old keg of rum!

Those happy days have passed away, I've seen their pleasures
  fade,
And many of our good old mates have with old times decayed.
But still, when on my travels, boys, I meet with an old chum,
We will sigh in conversation of the grand old keg of rum.

Chorus: The old keg of rum! the old keg of rum!
     We will sigh in conversation of the old keg of rum!

And now my song is ended, I've got to jog along,
An old buffer skiting of days dead and gone;
But you young coves who hear me will, perhaps, in years to
  come
Remember old Jack Palmer and his old keg of rum.

Chorus: The old keg of rum! the old keg of rum!
     Remember old Jack Palmer and his old keg of rum!

The Style in Which It's Done

Friend Draper steals ten thousand pounds,
   And gets three years in gaol;
While Devil Dick gets seventeen
   For sticking up the mail.
One punishment is over
   When the other's just begun,
Which shows how much depends upon
   The style in which it's done.

A Tail of a Kangaroo

It wasn't on the Chinee coast, nor yet upon Japan,
But happened on the Sydney side, not far from Marieyan –
As told me by a splitter, which his name is Blathering Jim,
A cove – you can't expect to get a lot of truth from him.

Chorus:
But there's no gammon in this yarn, for every word is true,
How maidens four waged deadly war with an old man kangaroo.

Within a hut of she-oak slabs, all roofed with stringybark,
Four Sydney-native ladies sat, all game for any lark.
Big Jane was there (Bondingie Bill, the bullock-driver's gal),
With Mountain Mag from Blue Lookout, and Parramatta Sal.

And Julia (whose bushranging brother Sam has come to grief)
Was cutting up and salting down a side of stolen beef,
While Mountain Mag was plaiting of a cracker from the thong
Of Jack, the boundary-rider's whip, that lives at Bogalong.

Big Jenny dreamt the happy hours away upon the bunk,
After an evening party, where no end of lush was drunk;
And Parramatta Sal, she blowed a tidy cloud of smoke,
While coiling in her possum rug, and thought about her bloke.

Her father, who was absent with his gully-raking sons,
Was busy duffing cattle on the nearest squatters' runs –
One of the good old colonists he was, who often bragged
That though he'd been quite close to it, he'd never yet been
    scragged.

'Twas thus these maidens, all alone, were mustered in the hut,
When on a sudden something bumped agin the door full butt;
Then Julia spoke, that artless maid brought up in nature's
    school,
'Don't stand there humbugging all day; come in, you – – fool!'

As no one answered to their call, on looking out, they saw
A booming kangaroo who'd run his head agin the door,
And being thus knocked out of time, and anxious for a swim,
Was making for the water, so the girls just went for him.

Now Julia's just the sort of girl to ride a bucking colt,
Or round a mob of cattle up, if they're inclined to bolt,
Ride on her brother's saddle all astride, or, on a push,
Do any mortal kind of work that's wanted in the bush.

And so she grabbed a roping-pole, and Maggie seized the adze,
With all her ringlets streaming loose with 'Follow me, my lads!'
The propstick of a bullock-dray was all that Jane could find,
But Sarah waved a waddy that the blacks had left behind.

On coming to close quarters with those formidable claws,
The 'old man' made for Sarah, but she hit him in the jaws,
As Julia gave the beggar fits, with that relentless arm
That cleared the shanty ballroom near the free-selector's farm.

Then, closing, he charged Marguerite, but missed her, so she
    placed
A stinger in the region of the middle of his waist,
And gave him such a mauling o'er the face, and eyes, and ribs,
As fellows do each other in these rowdy fighting cribs.

The boomah sought for vengeance, and grabbed Jenny by the
 skirt,
But luckily it gave, and so the lady wasn't hurt,
Though it must be confessed that she was terribly in dread,
Until the ladies rallied round, and knocked him on the head.

Thus 'old men' often come to grief, whene'er they chance to
 stray
Among the rocky gullies, where the ladies stop the way;
Because the girls are just as smart to bail up kangaroos,
As their parents are to travellers who've anything to lose.

The Squatter's Man

Come all ye lads an' list to me,
That's left your homes and crossed the sea,
To try your fortune, bond or free,
  All in this golden land.
For twelve long months I had to pace,
Humping my swag with a cadging face,
Sleeping in the bush, like the sable race,
  As in my song you'll understand.

Unto this country I did come,
A regular out-and-out new chum.
I then abhorred the sight of rum –
  Teetotal was my plan.
But soon I learned to wet one eye –
Misfortune often made me sigh.
To raise fresh funds I was forced to fly,
  And be a squatter's man.

Soon at a station I appeared.
I saw the squatter with his beard,
And up to him I boldly steered,
  With my swag and billy-can.

I said, 'Kind sir, I want a job!'
Said he, 'Do you know how to snob?
Or can you break in a bucking cob?'
   Whilst my figure he well did scan.

''Tis now I want a useful cove
To stop at home and not to rove.
The scamps go about – a regular drove –
   I 'spose you're one of the clan?
But I'll give ten – ten, sugar an' tea;
Ten bob a week if you'll suit me,
And very soon I hope you'll be
   A handy squatter's man.

'At daylight you must milk the cows,
Make butter, cheese, an' feed the sows,
Put on the kettle, the cook arouse,
   And clean the family shoes,
The stable an' sheep-yard clean out,
And always answer when we shout,
With "Yes, ma'am," "No, Sir!" Mind your mouth:
   And my youngsters don't abuse.

'You must fetch wood an' water, bake an' boil,
Act as butcher when we kill;
The corn an' taters you must hill,
   Keep the garden spick and span.
You must not scruple in the rain
To take to market all the grain.
Be sure you come sober back again
   To be a squatter's man.'

He sent me to an old bark hut,
Inhabited by a greyhound slut,
Who put her fangs through my poor fut,
   And, snarling, off she ran.

So once more I'm looking for a job,
Without a copper in my fob.
With Ben Hall or Gardiner I'd rather rob,
   Than be a squatter's man!

Lambed Down

The shades of night were falling fast,
As down a steep old gully passed
A man whom you could plainly see
Had just come off a drunken spree,
   Lambed down.

He'd left the station with his cheque,
And little evil did he reck;
At Ryan's pub he felt all right,
And yet he was, before next night,
   Lambed down.

'Oh, stay!' old Ryan said, 'and slip
Your blanket off, and have a nip;
I'll cash your cheque and send you on.'
He stopped, and now his money's gone –
   Lambed down.

He's got the shakes and thinks he sees
Blue devils lurking in the trees;
Oh, shearers! if you've any sense
Don't be on any such pretence
   Lambed down.

Bushman's Farewell to Queensland

Queensland, thou art a land of pests!
From flies and fleas one never rests,
Even now mosquitoes 'round me revel,
In fact they are the very devil.

Sand-flies and hornets just as bad,
They nearly drive a fellow mad:
The scorpion and centipede
With stinging ants of every breed.

Fever and ague with the shakes,
Tarantulas and poisonous snakes,
Goannas, lizards, cockatoos,
Bushrangers, logs and jackeroos.

Bandicoots and swarms of rats,
Bull-dog ants and native cats,
Stunted timber, thirsty plains,
Parched-up deserts, scanty rains.

There's rivers here you can't sail ships on,
There's nigger women without skirts on,
There's humpies, huts and wooden houses,
And nigger men who don't wear trousers.

There's Barcoo rot and sandy blight,
There's dingoes howling half the night,
There's curlews' wails and croaking frogs,
There's savage blacks and native dogs.

There's scentless flowers and stinging trees,
There's poison grass and Darling peas,
Which drive the cattle raving mad,
Make sheep and horses just as bad.

And then it never rains in reason.
There's drought one year and floods next season,
Which wash the squatters' sheep away,
And then there is the devil to pay.

To stay in thee, O land of Mutton!
I would not give a single button,
But bid thee now a long farewell,
Thou scorching sunburnt land of Hell!

ANON

In this period young and well-connected Englishmen were often sent out to Australia for 'colonial experience'. A Jackeroo lived, as a kind of gentleman apprentice, in the squatter's or manager's homestead, not in the men's huts; but most of his daily work was done side by side with the working 'hands'. Many satirical songs like this one were composed about those jackeroos who gave themselves airs.

Jimmy Sago, Jackeroo

If you want a situation, I'll just tell you the plan
To get on to a station, I am just your very man.
Pack up the old portmanteau, and label it Paroo,
With a name aristocratic – Jimmy Sago, Jackeroo.

When you get on to the station, of small things you'll make a
   fuss,
And in speaking of the station, mind, it's *we*, and *ours*, and *us*.
Boast of your grand connections and your rich relations, too,
And your own great expectations, Jimmy Sago, Jackeroo.

They will send you out on horseback, the boundaries to ride,
But run down a marsupial and rob him of his hide;
His scalp will fetch a shilling and his skin another two,
Which will help to fill your pockets, Jimmy Sago, Jackeroo.

When the boss wants information, on the men you'll do a
   sneak,
And don a paper collar on your fifteen bob a week.
Then at the lamb-marking a boss they'll make of you,
Now that's the way to get on, Jimmy Sago, Jackeroo!

A squatter in the future I've no doubt you may be,
But if the banks once get you, they'll put you up a tree.
To see you humping bluey, I know, would never do,
'Twould mean good-bye to our new chum, Jimmy Sago,
   Jackeroo.
Yes, good-bye to our new chum, Jimmy Sago, Jackeroo.

They've All Got a Mate but Me

There's the fox and the bear
And the dingo and the hare
And the birds in the greenwood tree,
  And there's the pretty little rabbits,
  So engaging in their habits,
They've all got a mate but me!

There's the emu on the flat
And the engaging little rat,
And the possum in the old gum tree:
  There's the goanna lying still
  And the wallaby on the hill –
Oh! They've all got a mate but me!

The Free Selectors' Song – 1861

Come all of you Cornstalks the victory's won,
John Robertson's triumphed, the lean days are gone.
No more through the bush we'll go humping the drum,
For the Land Bill has passed and the good times have come.

Chorus:
Then give me a hut in my own native land,
Or a tent in the bush, near the mountains so grand.
For the scenes of my childhood a joy are to me,
And the dear native girl who will share it with me.

No more through the bush with our swags need we roam,
For to ask of the squatters to give us a home.
Now the land is unfettered and we may reside,
In a place of our own by some clear waterside.

We will sow our own garden and till our own field,
And eat of the fruits that our labour doth yield,
And be independent, a right long denied,
By those who have ruled us and robbed us beside.

The Eumerella Shore

There's a happy little valley on the Eumerella shore,
   Where I've lingered many hours away;
On my little free selection I have acres by the score,
   Where I unyoke the bullocks from the dray.

Chorus:
   To my bullocks then I say:
   No matter where you stray,
     You will never be impounded any more;
For you're running, running, running on the duffer's piece of
     land,
   Free-selected on the Eumerella shore.

When the moon has climbed the mountains and the stars are
     shining bright,
   Then we saddle up our horses and away,
And we'll duff the squatter's cattle in the darkness of the night,
   And we'll have the calves all branded by the day.

Chorus:
   Oh, my pretty little calf,
   At the squatter you may laugh,
     For he'll never be your owner any more;
For you're running, running, running on the duffer's piece of
     land,
   Free-selected on the Eumerella shore.

If we find a mob of horses when the paddock rails are down,
   Although before they're never known to stray,
Oh, quickly will we drive them to some distant inland town,
   And sell them into slavery far away.

Chorus:
   To Jack Robertson we'll say,
   You've been leading us astray,
     And we'll never go a-farming any more;
For it's easier duffing cattle on the little piece of land,
   Free-selected on the Eumerella shore.

ROWLAND SKEMP (1863-1947)

Born in Shropshire, Skemp emigrated to Tasmania at the age of twenty. With his brother he took up a bush selection at Myrtle Bank in the north-eastern part of the island and remained there as a farmer for the rest of his life. From his letters and papers an interesting biography, *Memories of Myrtle Bank*, was compiled by his son, J.R. Skemp.

The Cocky Farmer

O listen to the sorrows of a cocky farmer sad,
   Who tried to make his living in the bush.
When he first went into farming, oh, his heart was proud and
     glad,
   For he thought that now his fortune he could push,
When he started in the forest he exclaimed with accents gay,
   'I shall soon have made a home for darling Jane,
I can clear the scrub and timber by the acre in the day,
   And I'll soon have houses, barns and fields of grain.'

Chorus:
   But now his hopes are blighted,
   She to whom his faith was plighted
   His loving heart has slighted,
Now she's found that he is poor!

Oh, he sowed the land with grasses and he planted many spuds,
   With thistles fine and turnips, oats and wheat;
And he bought him forty sheep and twenty ancient cows,
   And twenty little pigs to give him meat.
But the grubs ate all his grass and the rain spoilt all his hay
   While his pigs ate all his spuds and turnips round.
And it cost him fifteen sovereigns when his cattle got astray,
   Just to rescue them from out the public pound.

Then he sheared his sheep in winter and they all died in the
    spring,
  And one by one his pigs all pined away,
While his cattle died of measles and his poultry all took wing
  To that better land we hope to see some day.

So he made a little graveyard and he dug a row of graves;
  There he planted all his stock beneath the ground.
And he printed on a paling that he fastened to the fence –
  'Here lies all my stock but one that's in the pound.'

In that spot his hopes lies buried; far beneath the green grass
    turf
  Twenty ancient cows he laid below,
And forty sheep and poultry, and his cats and dogs beside,
  And twenty little porkers in a row.
Then he sold his land by auction and he 'saw the money out',
  And even yet, although he's sent the 'chink',
Still in beer he drowns his sorrows when he finds a friend
    who'll shout
  And his tale of woe he'll tell for just one drink.

IV

(1861-85)

EARLY LITERARY BALLADISTS

MOST of the early ballads about Australian life were anonymously made by common folk. The small minority of cultivated colonists naturally tended for several generations to write about England. Even when they sought to describe the daily life around them they tended to see it through the borrowed spectacles of English literary convention. In the sixties and seventies, however, a few Australian literary men began to write an occasional poem in which they sought to describe bush life realistically.

Most of the writers in this section, as their verses show, felt that daily life in Australia was hardly a proper subject for serious poetry: though well enough, perhaps, to furnish matter for an occasional exercise in light verse-making. When they escaped this condescending approach they tended, like Barcroft Boake, to adopt an opposite but hardly less embarrassing air of self-conscious, tragic grimness. Nevertheless, some of these literary exercises paved the way for the true bush ballads of following decades.

HENRY KENDALL (1839-82)

Grandson of a missionary who had been granted land in New South Wales in the early days, Henry Kendall spent most of his life in the coastal forest and dairy-farming country on the north and south coasts of that colony. Drink and poverty dogged the life of both his parents and made his own life more wretched, in many ways, than it need have been. Yet he enjoyed the appreciation and friendship of a few discerning contemporaries.

He was probably the most considerable Australian poet of the nineteenth century, though some judges would argue the claims of Harpur and Gordon. The jocular air of *Jim the Splitter* is quite foreign to most of Kendall's verse.

Jim the Splitter

The bard who is singing of Wollombi Jim
Is hardly just now in the requisite trim
   To sit on his Pegasus fairly;
Besides, he is bluntly informed by the Muse
That Jim is a subject no singer should choose;
   For Jim is poetical rarely.

But being full up of the myths that are Greek –
Of the classic, and noble, and nude, and antique,
   Which means not a rag but the pelt on;
This poet intends to give Daphne the slip,
For the sake of a hero in moleskin and kip
   With a jumper and snake-buckle belt on.

No party is Jim of the Pericles type –
He is modern right up from the toe to the pipe;
   And being no reader or roamer,
He hasn't Euripides much in the head;
And let it be carefully, tenderly said,
   He never has analyzed Homer.

He can roar out a song of the twopenny kind;
But, knowing the beggar so well, I'm inclined
   To believe that a 'par.' about Kelly,
The rascal who skulked under shadow of curse,
Is more in his line than the happiest verse
   On the glittering pages of Shelley.

You mustn't, however, adjudge him in haste,
Because a red robber is more to his taste
   Than Ruskin, Rossetti, or Dante!
You see, he was bred in a bangalow wood,
And bangalow pith was the principal food
   His mother served out in her shanty.

His knowledge is this – he can tell in the dark,
What timber will split by the feel of the bark;
   And rough as his manner of speech is,
His wits to the fore he can readily bring
In passing off ash as the genuine thing
   When scarce in the forest the beech is.

In girthing a tree that he sells in the round,
He assumes, as a rule, that the body is sound,
   And measures, forgetting to bark it!
He may be a ninny, but still the old dog
Can plug to perfection a pipe of a log
   And palm it away on the market.

He splits a fair shingle, but holds to the rule
Of his father's, and, haply, his grandfather's school;
   Which means that he never has blundered,
When tying his shingles, by slinging in more
Than the recognized number of ninety and four
   To the bundle he sells for a hundred!

When asked by the market for ironbark red,
It always occurs to the Wollombi head
   To do a 'mahogany' swindle.
In forests where never the ironbark grew,
When Jim is at work, it would flabbergast you
   To see how the ironbarks dwindle.

He can stick to the saddle, can Wollombi Jim,
And when a buckjumper dispenses with him,
   The leather goes off with the rider.
And, as to a team, over gully and hill
He can travel with twelve on the breadth of a quill
   And boss the unlucky offsider.

He shines at his best at the tiller of saw,
On the top of the pit, where his whisper is law
   To the gentleman working below him.

When the pair of them pause in a circle of dust,
Like a monarch he poses – exalted, august –
　　There's nothing this planet can show him!

For a man is a *man* who can sharpen and set,
And *he* is the only thing masculine yet
　　According to sawyer and splitter –
Or rather according to Wollombi Jim;
And nothing will tempt me to differ from him,
　　For Jim is a bit of a hitter.

But, being full up, we'll allow him to rip,
Along with his lingo, his saw, and his whip –
　　He isn't the classical notion.
And, after a night in his humpy, you see
A person of orthodox habits would be
　　Refreshed by a dip in the ocean.

To tot him right up from the heel to the head,
He isn't the Grecian of whom we have read –
　　His face is a trifle too shady.
The nymph in green valleys of Thessaly dim
Would never jack up her old lover for him,
　　For she has the tastes of a lady.

So much for our hero! A statuesque foot
Would suffer by wearing the heavy-nailed boot –
　　Its owner is hardly Achilles.
However, he's happy! He cuts a great fig
In the land where a coat is no part of the rig –
　　In the country of damper and billies.

'ALEXANDER FORBES'

This was the pen-name under which William Anderson Forbes published a slim volume of poems, *Voices from the Bush*, in Rockhampton, Queensland, in 1869. Son of a Presbyterian minister in northern Scotland, and younger brother of the well-known war correspondent, Archibald Forbes, William is said to have been sent down from the university 'for a madcap piece of youthful folly'. He ran away to sea and then spent the rest of his life as an itinerant bushworker in Queensland. To judge from this poem, he worked as a shepherd on an outback station for some time with a Chinese mate as 'hut-keeper'. He died in Toowoomba before the turn of the century.

The Mandarin from China

Now friends if you'll attention pay,
    And list to what I state;
I'm certain you will pity feel
    For my unhappy fate.
For here I am in Queensland's bush,
    An awful sight to see,
And a Mandarin from China
    To keep company with me.

My humpy, from its looks was built
    Soon after Noah's ark,
Roof, sides, and gable all composed
    Of rotten sheets of bark.
On rainy days, the heavy wet
    Comes pouring down quite free,
On the Mandarin from China,
    But alas likewise on me.

Ye gods! to think that one whose sires
    At Bannockburn have bled,
Must now associate with a man,
    In China born and bred.

From the brave old 'land of cakes' I hail,
   While from the realms of tea
Comes the Mandarin from China,
   That keeps company with me.

In shape his lovely frontispiece
   Resembles much the moon,
His mouth is like the Cove of Cork,
   His nose is like a spoon.
A liver-coloured, whitey-brown,
   Magenta skin has he,
This Mandarin from China
   That keeps company with me.

His lingo is most horrible,
   To listen gives much pain;
So I have a code of signals framed
   His meaning to explain.
My English puzzles him no doubt,
   God knows, his, puzzles me,
Which makes this man from China
   Most indifferent company.

The place of his nativity,
   I'm sure I cannot tell;
'Tis no great loss, for if I knew,
   Its name I could not spell.
Some crackjaw words, you may depend,
   Are in the pedigree,
Of the Mandarin from China
   That keeps company with me.

But still he has some first-rate points,
   As who on earth has not;
Celestial is the way he works
   The frying-pan and pot.
A splendid feed can be produced
   While you'd be counting three,
By the Mandarin from China
   That keeps company with me.

To fetch up wood and water too
   He never will refuse,
But, yet, if I could have my way,
   Another mate I'd choose.
With whom, I feel quite confident,
   I better could agree,
Than with the Mandarin from China
   That keeps company with me.

ADAM LINDSAY GORDON (1833-70)

Son of a retired Indian Army officer, Gordon was born in the Azores Islands and educated at Cheltenham College and the Woolwich Military Academy. He showed little interest in formal studies and was sent to Australia 'because of his waywardness' in 1853. In South Australia he was successively a mounted policeman, a horse-breaker, and for two years a member of the colonial parliament. In 1868 he moved to Melbourne but committed suicide there on the day of publication of his fourth book of verse, *Bush Ballads and Galloping Rhymes*. There is a tablet to his memory in Westminster Abbey.

The Sick Stockrider, which appeared in this book, is one of the very few pieces in which he turned his hand to the Australian scene. For this reason, and because it anticipates in spirit so much of the 'bush ballad' verse which began to be published twenty years later, *The Sick Stockrider* has always been easily his most popular poem.

The Sick Stockrider

Hold hard, Ned! Lift me down once more, and lay me in the
   shade.
   Old man, you've had your work cut out to guide
Both horses, and to hold me in the saddle when I sway'd
   All through the hot, slow, sleepy, silent ride.
The dawn at 'Moorabinda' was a mist rack dull and dense,
   The sunrise was a sullen, sluggish lamp;
I was dozing in the gateway at Arbuthnot's bound'ry fence,
   I was dreaming on the Limestone cattle camp.

We crossed the creek at Carricksford, and sharply through the
   haze,
   And suddenly the sun shot flaming forth;
To southward lay 'Katawa' with the sand peaks all ablaze
   And the flush'd fields of Glen Lomond lay to north.

Now westward winds the bridle path that leads to Lindisfarm,
   And yonder looms the double-headed Bluff;
From the far side of the first hill, when the skies are clear and
     calm,
   You can see Sylvester's woolshed fair enough.

Five miles we used to call it from our homestead to the place
   Where the big tree spans the roadway like an arch;
'Twas here we ran the dingo down that gave us such a chase
   Eight years ago – or was it nine? – last March.
'Twas merry in the glowing morn, among the gleaming grass
   To wander as we've wander'd many a mile,
And blow the cool tobacco cloud, and watch the white wreaths
     pass,
   Sitting loosely in the saddle all the while.

'Twas merry mid the blackwoods when we spied the station
     roofs,
   To wheel the wild scrub cattle at the yard,
With a running fire of stockwhips and a fiery run of hoofs;
   Oh! the hardest day was never then too hard!
Ay! we had a glorious gallop after 'Starlight' and his gang,
   When they bolted from Sylvester's on the flat;
How the sun-dried reed-beds crackled, how the flint-strewn
     rangs rang
   To the strokes of 'Mountaineer' and 'Acrobat!'

Hard behind them in the timber, harder still across the heath,
   Close beside them through the tea-tree scrub we dash'd;
And the golden-tinted fern leaves, how they rustled underneath!
   And the honeysuckle osiers, how they crash'd!
We led the hunt throughout, Ned, on the chestnut and the grey,
   And the troopers were three hundred yards behind,
While we emptied our six-shooters on the bushrangers at bay,
   In the creek with stunted box-tree for a blind!

There you grappled with the leader, man to man and horse to
　　horse,
　　And you roll'd together when the chestnut rear'd;
He blazed away and missed you in that shallow water course –
　　A narrow shave – his powder singed your beard!
In these hours when life is ebbing, how those days when life
　　was young
　　Come back to us; how clearly I recall
Even the yarns Jack Hall invented, and the songs Jem Roper
　　sung;
　　And where are now Jem Roper and Jack Hall?

Ay! nearly all our comrades of the old colonial school,
　　Our ancient boon companions, Ned, are gone;
Hard livers for the most part, somewhat reckless as a rule,
　　It seems that you and I are left alone.
There was Hughes, who got in trouble through that business
　　with the cards,
　　It matters little what became of him;
But a steer ripp'd up Macpherson in the Cooraminta yards,
　　And Sullivan was drown'd at Sink-or-Swim.

And Mostyn – poor Frank Mostyn – died at last a fearful
　　wreck,
　　In 'the horrors,' at the Upper Wandinong,
And Carisbrooke, the rider, at the Horsefall broke his neck,
　　Faith! the wonder was he saved his neck so long!
Ah! those days and nights we squandered at the Logans' in
　　the glen –
　　The Logans, man and wife, have long been dead.
Elsie's tallest girl seems taller than your little Elsie then;
　　And Ethel is a woman grown and wed.

I've had my share of pastime, and I've done my share of toil,
　　And life is short – the longest life a span;
I care not now to tarry for the corn or for the oil,
　　Or for the wine that maketh glad the heart of man.

For good undone and gifts misspent and resolutions vain,
  'Tis somewhat late to trouble. This I know –
I should live the same life over, if I had to live again;
  And the chances are I go where most men go.

The deep blue skies wax dusky and the tall green trees grow
    dim,
  The sward beneath me seems to heave and fall;
And sickly, smoky shadows through the sleepy sunlight swim,
  And on the very sun's face weave their pall.
Let me slumber in the hollow where the wattle blossoms wave,
  With never stone or rail to fence my bed;
Should the sturdy station children pull the bush flowers on my
    grave,
  I may chance to hear them romping overhead.

E. W. HORNUNG (1866-1921)

Hornung is best remembered for his stories about the gentleman-burglar, Raffles. He spent only three years, from 1884 to 1886, in Australia, but most of his many novels make more or less use of his knowledge of the country. Even Raffles begins his career of crime while visiting Australia as a member of the first visiting English cricket team. The accurate knowledge of the old bushman's ritualistic method of 'lambing down' his cheque, which this poem displays, was probably acquired during the author's sojourn as a tutor on a station at Mossgiel in the western Riverina (N.S.W.).

The Stockman's Cheque

There's a hut in Riverina where a solitary hand
May weaken on himself and all that's his;
There's a pub in Riverina where they keep a smashing brand
Of every sort of liquor short o' fizz.
And I've been an' blued another fifty-pounder at the pub –
You're very sorry for me, I'll be bound!
But when a man is fit up free with hut, an' horse, an' grub,
What the blazes does he want with fifty pound?

Why the devil should he hoard his fifty quid?
Who would be a bit the better if he did?
Though they slithered in a week,
When I couldn't see or speak,
Do you think I'm here to squeak?
    Lord forbid.

The boss was in the homestead: when he give me good advice
I took my oath, but took his cheque as well.
And to me the moonlit shanty looked a pocket paradise,
Though the boss had just been calling it a hell.
Then the shanty-keeper's daughter, she's an educated lass,
And she bangs the new pianner all for me;
And the shanty-keeper's wife she sticks me up as bold as brass,
An' the shanty-keeper's wife is good to see.

Two petticoats between 'em whisk you far!
But the shanty-keeper smoked behind the bar.
Oh, his words were grave and few,
And he never looked at you,
But he just uncorked a new
    Gallon jar.

We fed and then we started in the bar at nine o'clock;
At twelve we made a move into the cool;
The shanty-keeper *he* was just as steady as a rock,
And me as paralytic as a fool.
I remember the veranda like a sinkin' vessel's deck,
And a brace of moons suspended in the sky . . .
And nothing more till waking and inquiring for my cheque,
And the oath of all them three I'd drunk it dry!

So that was all I got for fifty notes!
The three of 'em stood lying in their throats:
There was one that must have seen
I'd have beat him blue an' green
If I hadn't gone an' been
    Off my oats.

Thank the Lord I'm back at last – though back-wrecked and
    whisky-logged!
Yet the gates have not come open that I shut,
And I've seen no broken fences, and I've found no weak sheep
    bogged,
An' my little cat is purring in the hut.
There's tea, too, for the billy-can, there's water in the tanks,
The ration-bags hang heavy all around;
An' my good old bunk an' blanket beat the bare veranda
    planks
Of the shanty where I blued my fifty pound!

Here I stick until I'm worth fifty more,
When I'll take another cheque from the stor
And with Riverina men
All the betting is that then
I shall knock it down again
    As before.

GEORGE ESSEX EVANS (1863-1909)

Born in London, Evans took up farming in Queensland in 1881.
When his farm failed he took up school-teaching and journalism
before he found permanent employment in the Queensland
Public Service. Most of his verse is conventionally meditative or
descriptive in the manner of *The Women of the West*. *A Drought
Idyll* is, for Evans, a rare excursion into the more popular
ballad field.

The Women of the West

They left the vine-wreathed cottage and the mansion on the hill,
The houses in the busy streets where life is never still,
The pleasures of the city, and the friends they cherished best:
For love they faced the wilderness – the Women of the West.

The roar, and rush, and fever of the city died away,
And the old-time joys and faces – they were gone for many a
    day;
In their place the lurching coach-wheel, or the creaking
    bullock chains,
O'er the everlasting sameness of the never-ending plains.

In the slab-built, zinc-roofed homestead of some lately-taken
    run,
In the tent beside the bankment of a railway just begun,
In the huts on new selections, in the camps of man's unrest,
On the frontiers of the Nation, live the Women of the West.

The red sun robs their beauty, and, in weariness and pain,
The slow years steal the nameless grace that never comes again;
And there are hours men cannot soothe, and words men cannot
    say –
The nearest woman's face may be a hundred miles away.

The wide Bush holds the secrets of their longings and desires,
When the white stars in reverence light their holy altar-fires,
And silence, like the touch of God, sinks deep into the breast –
Perchance He hears and understands the Women of the West.

For them no trumpet sounds the call, no poet plies his arts –
They only hear the beating of their gallant, loving hearts.
But they have sung with silent lives the song all songs above –
The holiness of sacrifice, the dignity of love.

Well have we held our father's creed. No call has passed us by.
We faced and fought the wilderness, we sent our sons to die.
And we have hearts to do and dare, and yet, o'er all the rest,
The hearts that made the Nation were the Women of the West.

A Drought Idyll

It was the middle of the drought; the ground was hot and bare,
You might search for grass with a microscope, but 'nary grass
    was there;
The hay was done, the cornstalks gone, the trees were dying
    fast.
The sun o'erhead was a curse in red, and the wind was a
    furnace blast;
The waterholes were sun-baked mud, the drays stood thick
    as bees
Around the well, a mile away, amid the ring-barked trees.

McGinty left his pumpkin-pie and gazed upon the scene:
His cows stood propped 'gainst tree and fence wherever they
    could lean;
The horse he'd fixed with sapling-forks had fallen down once
    more;
The fleas were hopping joyfully on stockyard, path, and floor;
The flies in thousands buzzed about before his waving hand;
The hungry pigs squealed as he said, 'Me own, me native land!'

'Queensland, me Mother! Ain't yer well?' he asked. 'Come'
    tell me how's –'
'Dry up! Dry up!' yelled Mrs Mac, 'Go out and feed the cows.'
'But where's the feed?' McGinty cried, 'The sugar-cane's all
    done –
It wasn't worth the bally freight we paid for it per ton.
I'll get me little axe and go with Possum and the mare
For 'arf-a-ton of apple-tree or a load of prickly-pear.'

'The prickly-pear'll kill the cows unless yer bile it right,'
Cried Mrs Mac, 'and I don't mean to bile it all the night.
They tell me fer a bob a bag the brewery will sell
Their refuse stuff, like Simpson 'ad, – His cows is doin' well.
Yer get the loan of Bampston's dray and borrer Freeney's nags,
And fetch along a decent load, McGinty – thirty bags.'

McGinty borrowed Bampston's dray and hitched up Freeney's
    nags,
And drove like blazes into town and fetched back thirty bags.
The stuff was mellow, soft and brown; and if you came too
    near
It shed around a lovely scent till the air seemed full of *beer*.
McGinty fetched each feed-box out and filled it to the brim,
Then lit his pipe and fell asleep. That was the style of him!

The cows, they lurched off fence and tree and staggered in to
    feed,
The horses tottered after them – old, feeble, and knock-kneed.
But when they smelt that sacred stuff in boxes on the ground
They smiled and neighed and low'd and twirled their hungry
    tails around.
You would have walked a hundred miles or more to see and
    hear
The way McGinty's stock attacked that stuff that smelt like
    beer.

*

'Wake up! Wake up! McGinty man! Wake up!' yelled Mrs
    Mac.
She held a broom and every word was followed by a whack.
McGinty had been dreaming hard that it was Judgment Day
And he was drafted with the goats and being driven away.
The Devil with a toasting fork was jabbing at his jaw,
He rose and yelled and fled outside – and this is what he saw:

The brindle cow, with spotted tail, was trying to climb a tree;
The spotted cow, with brindle tail, to imitate a flea;
Old Bally who had lost one horn engaged in combat stout
With the Lincoln ram whose only eye McGinty had knocked
    out;
With tails entwined, among the trees, went Bessie and Basilk,
Singing, 'Good-bye, McGinty, we will come back with the
    milk.'

McGinty, trembling, viewed the scene in wonderment and funk,
Then lifted up his voice and roared, 'Mother, the cows is drunk!
Look at that bloomin' heifer with 'er head 'ung down the sty,
Telling the sow she loves 'er but she some'ow can't tell why.
Three of 'em snoring on their backs, the rest all on the loose –
Ain't there no policeman in these parts when cows get on the
    booze?'

McGinty viewed the orgy with a jealousy profound.
Cows in various states of drunk were scattered all around;
But most his rage was heightened by the conduct of his horse
That stood and laughed, and laughed, and laughed – and
    laughed without remorse –
That horse so oft he'd lifted up and propped with logs and
    boughs
Now leant against a tree and mocked McGinty and his cows.

'Bring soda-water, Mother,' cried McGinty. 'Bring a tub,'
(Forgetting that he lived about a league from any pub.)
'I swear by soda-water when the drink illumes my brow,
And if it fixes up a man it ought to fix a cow.'
But as he spoke a boozy steer approached with speed intense
And helped McGinty over to the safe side of the fence.

Regret and hate and envy held McGinty where he sat.
'To think,' he said, 'these purple cows should have a time
    like that!
For months I couldn't raise a drink – it wasn't up to me;
Yet every bally head of stock I've got is on the spree.
This comes when you forget to keep a bottle on the shelf.'

*

Inspired, he rose and smote his brow and fetched a spoon
    and delf –

*

'My word!' he said, 'It's up to me to feed on this meself!'

MARY HANNAY FOOTT (1846-1918)

Mary Black, born in Glasgow, came to Australia at the age of six and was educated in Melbourne and at the National Gallery Art School there. In 1874 she married Thomas Foott, manager and part-owner of an outback station in south-western Queensland on the Paroo River where she went to live.

This popular poem refers to a legendary land of promise beyond the farthest-out western runs, which lured many pioneers to their deaths.

Where the Pelican Builds Her Nest

The horses were ready, the rails were down,
But the riders lingered still –
One had a parting word to say,
And one had his pipe to fill.
Then they mounted, one with a granted prayer,
And one with a grief unguessed.
'We are going,' they said, as they rode away –
'Where the pelican builds her nest!'

They had told us of pastures wide and green,
To be sought past the sunset's glow;
Of rifts in the ranges by opal lit;
And gold 'neath the river's flow.
And thirst and hunger were banished words
When they spoke of that unknown West;
No drought they dreaded, no flood they feared.
Where the pelican builds her nest!

The creek at the ford was but fetlock deep
When we watched them crossing there;
The rains have replenished it thrice since then,
And thrice has the rock lain bare.
But the waters of Hope have flowed and fled,
And never from blue hill's breast
Come back – by the sun and the sands devoured –
Where the pelican builds her nest!

Born in Sydney, Boake's short life was spent in surveying, drov-
ing, boundary-riding, and other bush work. He hanged himself
with the lash of his stockwhip when he was only 26 years old.
Like Mary Hannay Foott he avoids the note of condescension
which mars the work of some other early balladists; but suffers
from an opposite weakness. For him bush life is almost uniformly
grim, bitter and tragic – which it was not, as the later balladists
knew, though Lawson was often in danger of forgetting it.

Where the Dead Men Lie

Out on the wastes of the Never Never –
   That's where the dead men lie!
There where the heat-waves dance for ever –
   That's where the dead men lie!
That's where the Earth's loved sons are keeping
Endless Tryst: not the west wind sweeping
Feverish pinions can wake their sleeping –
   Out where the dead men lie!

Where brown Summer and Death have mated –
   That's where the dead men lie!
Loving with fiery lust unsated –
   That's where the dead men lie!
Out where the grinning skulls bleach whitely
Under the saltbush sparkling brightly;
Out where the wild dogs chorus nightly –
   That's where the dead men lie!

Deep in the yellow, flowing river –
   That's where the dead men lie!
Under the banks where the shadows quiver –
   That's where the dead men lie!
Where the platypus twists and doubles,
Leaving a train of tiny bubbles;
Rid at last of their earthly troubles –
   That's where the dead men lie!

East and backward pale faces turning –
   That's how the dead men lie!
Gaunt arms stretched with a voiceless yearning –
   That's how the dead men lie!
Oft in the fragrant hush of nooning
Hearing again their mother's crooning,
Wrapt for aye in a dreamful swooning –
   That's how the dead men lie!

Only the hand of Night can free them –
   That's when the dead men fly!
Only the frightened cattle see them –
   See the dead men go by!
Cloven hoofs beating out one measure,
Bidding the stockmen know no leisure –
That's when the dead men take their pleasure!
   That's when the dead men fly!

Ask, too, the never-sleeping drover:
   He sees the dead pass by;
Hearing them call to their friends – the plover,
   Hearing the dead men cry;
Seeing their faces stealing, stealing,
Hearing their laughter, pealing, pealing,
Watching their grey forms wheeling, wheeling
   Round where the cattle lie!

Strangled by thirst and fierce privation –
   That's how the dead men die!
Out on Moneygrub's farthest station –
   That's how the dead men die!
Hard-faced greybeards, youngsters callow;
Some mounds cared for, some left fallow;
Some deep down, yet others shallow;
   Some having but the sky.

Moneygrub, as he sips his claret,
   Looks with complacent eye
Down at his watch-chain, eighteen carat
   There, in his club, hard by:
Recks not that every link is stamped with
Names of men whose limbs are cramped with
Too long lying in grave-mould, cramped with
   Death where the dead men lie.

ARTHUR PATCHETT MARTIN (1851-1902)

Born in England but brought to Melbourne as a babe in arms during the second year of the Gold Rush, Martin took an active part in the journalistic and literary life of Melbourne until his departure for England in 1882.

Australian (and other readers outside the United Kingdom) should note that Pall Mall is pronounced 'Pell Mell'.

My Cousin from Pall Mall

There's nothing so exasperates a true Australian youth,
Whatever be his rank in life, be he cultured or uncouth,
As the manner of a London swell. Now it chanced, the other day,
That one came out, consigned to me – a cousin, by the way

As he landed from the steamer at the somewhat dirty pier,
He took my hand; and lispingly remarked, 'How very queer!
I'm glad, of course, to see you – but you must admit this place,
With all its mixed surroundings, is a national disgrace.'

I defended not that dirty pier, not a word escaped my lips;
I pointed not – though well I might – to the huge three-masted ships;
For, although with patriotic pride my soul was all aglow,
I remembered Trollope's parting words, 'Victorians do not blow.'

On the morrow through the city we sauntered, arm in arm;
I strove to do the cicerone – my style was grand and calm.
I showed him all the lions – but I noted with despair
His smile, his drawl, his eye-glass, and his supercilious air.

As we strolled along that crowded street, where Fashion holds proud sway,
He deigned to glance at every thing, but not one word did say;
I really thought he was impressed by its well-deserved renown
Till he drawled, 'Not bad – not bad at all – for a provincial town.'

Just as he spoke there chanced to pass a most bewitching girl,
And I said, 'Dear cousin, is she not fit bride for any earl?'
He glanced, with upraised eyebrows and a patronizing smile,
Then lisped, 'She's pretty, not a doubt, but what a want of
    style!'

We paused a moment just before a spacious House of Prayer;
Said he, 'Dear me! Good gracious! What's this ugly brick
    affair –
A second-rate gin-palace?' 'Cease, cease,' I said; 'you must –
O spare me,' – here my sobs burst forth, I was humbled to the
    dust.

But, unmindful of my agonies, in the slowest of slow drawls,
He lisped away for hours of the Abbey and St Paul's,
Till those grand historic names had for me a hateful sound,
And I wished the noble piles themselves were levelled to the
    ground,

My young bright life seemed blasted, my hopes were dead and
    gone,
No blighted lover ever felt so gloomy and forlorn;
I'd reached the suicidal stage – and the reason of it all,
This supercilious London swell, his eye-glass and his drawl.

But, though hidden, still there's present, in our darkest hour
    of woe,
A sense of respite and relief, although we may not know
The way that gracious Providence will choose to right the
    wrong,
So I forthwith ceased my bitter tears – I suffered and was strong.

Then we strolled into the Club, where he again commenced
    to speak,
But I interrupted saying, 'Let us leave town for a week.
I see that Melbourne bores you – nay, nay, I know it's true;
Let us wander 'midst the gum-trees, and observe the kangaroo.'

My words were soft and gentle, and none could have discerned
How, beneath my calm demeanour, volcanic fury burned.
And my cousin straight consented, as his wine he slowly sipped,
To see the gay Marsupial and the gloomy Eucalypt.

Ah! who has ever journeyed on a glorious summer night
Through the weird Australian bush-land without feeling of
    delight?
The dense untrodden forest, in the moonlight coldly pale,
Brings before our wondering eyes again the scenes of fairy tale.

No sound is heard, save where one treads upon the lonely
    track;
We lose our dull grey manhood, and to early youth go back –
To scenes and days long passed away, and seem again to greet
Our youthful dreams, so rudely crushed like the grass beneath
    our feet.

'Twas such a night we wandered forth; we never spoke a word
(I was too full of thought for speech – to him no thought
    occurred)
When, gazing from the silent earth to the star-lit silent sky,
My cousin in amazement dropped his eye-glass from his eye.

At last, I thought his soul was moved by the grandeur of the
    scene
(As the most prosaic Colonist's I'm certain would have been),
Till he replaced his eye-glass, and remarked – 'This may be
    well,
But one who's civilized prefers the pavement of Pall Mall.'

*

I swerved not from that moment from my purpose foul and
    grim;
I never deigned to speak one word, nor even glanced at him;
But suddenly I seized his throat, ... he gave one dreadful
    groan,
And I, who had gone forth with him, that night returned alone.

V

(1885–1914)

TRADITIONAL BUSH BALLADS

ANONYMOUS folk-songs, tales, and recitations were made in plenty by common bush-dwellers long before the last decade or two of the nineteenth century, as we have seen in previous sections of this book: but comparatively few of them have survived.

In this section we give a small selection of some of the most authentic and colourful songs and rhymes, made 'by the Lord Knows Who', during the fifteen years or so on both sides of the year of federation, 1901, a period when the Australian bush ballad flourished as never before or since.

The reader may decide for himself whether Lawson, Paterson, and the other 'literary' bush balladists of the period owed more to these anonymous singers than they did to the 'literary' ballad precursors whose work has been exemplified in the last section. It should be remembered, however, that many of the anonymous songs in this section did not pre-date the first published work of Lawson and Paterson. Some of them, like *The Spider by the Gwydir*, almost certainly were composed after Lawson's and Paterson's work had become very popular. The last item in the section, *McQuade's Curse*, was collected in 1962 though it almost certainly has an ancient folk-lineage. The *Curse* was pinned to the railway-gates in the Victorian country town of Tallarook, by a swagman who had been refused a drink of rum on credit at one of the town's hotels. *Lalla Rookh* was the name of an immensely popular verse-romance by Leigh Hunt (1784–1859), and Father Matthew was a celebrated Irish temperance advocate of the same period.

The Ramble-eer

The earth rolls on through empty space, its journey's never
   done;
It's entered through a starry race throughout the kingdom-
   come.
And, as I am a bit of earth, I follow it because –
And to prove I am a rolling stone and never gather moss.

Chorus:
For I am a ramble-eer, a rollicking ramble-eer,
I'm a roving rake of poverty, and son-of-a-gun for beer.

I've done a bit of fossicking for tucker and for gold;
I've been a menial rouseabout and a rollicking shearer bold.
I've 'shanked' across the Old Man Plain, after busting up a
   cheque
And 'whipped the cat' once more again, though I haven't
   met it yet.

I've done a bit of droving of cattle and of sheep,
And I've done a bit of moving with 'Matilda' for a mate;
Of fencing I have done my share, wool-scouring on the green,
Axeman, navvy. Old Nick can bear me out in what I haven't
   been.

I've worked the treadmill-thresher, the scythe and reaping-
   hook,
Been wood-and-water fetcher for Mary Jane the cook;
I've done a few 'cronk' things too, when I have struck a town,
There's a few things I wouldn't do – but I never did 'lambing
   down.'

Lazy Harry's

Oh! we started out from Roto, when the sheds had all cut out.
We'd whips and whips of rhino, and we meant to push about;
So we humped our blues serenely and made for Sydney town,
With a three-spot cheque between us, as wanted knocking
   down.

Chorus:

But we camped at Lazy Harry's, on the road to Gundagai,
The road to Gundagai! Not five miles from Gundagai!
Yes, we camped at Lazy Harry's, on the road to Gundagai.

Well, we struck the Murrumbidgee near the Yanko in a week,
And passed through old Narrandera and crossed the Burnet
    Creek;
And we never stopped at Wagga, for we'd Sydney in our eye,
But we camped at Lazy Harry's, on the road to Gundagai.

Oh! I've seen a lot of girls, my boys, and drunk a lot of beer,
And I've met with some of both, chaps, as has left me mighty
    queer;
But for beer to knock you sideways, and for girls to make you
    cry,
You must camp at Lazy Harry's, on the road to Gundagai.

Well, we chucked our bloomin' swags off, and we walked into
    the bar,
And we called for rum and raspb'ry and a shilling-each cigar,
But the girl that served the poison, she winked at Bill and I,
And we camped at Lazy Harry's, not five miles from Gundagai.

In a week the spree was over, and the cheque was all knocked
    down;
So we shouldered our matildas, and we turned our backs on
    town;
But the girls they stood a nobbler as we sadly waved 'Good-
    bye',
And we tramped from Lazy Harry's, not five miles from
    Gundagai.

Chorus:

Yes we tramped from Lazy Harry's, on the road to Gundagai,
The road to Gundagai! Not five miles from Gundagai!
Yes we tramped from Lazy Harry's, on the road to Gundagai.

Lousy Harry

Come boys, let's yoke the horses up
  And make an early start;
The roads are rough and heavy,
  Each one must do his part.

We must travel in the morning
  While the weather it is cool,
And we'll camp with Lousy Harry
  On the road to Carrathool.

Harry lives on bread and treacle,
  You'll find he is no fool;
They call him Lousy Harry
  On the road to Carrathool.

Click Go the Shears

Out on the board the old shearer stands,
Grasping his shears in his long, bony hands;
Fixed is his gaze on a bare-bellied yeo,
Glory if he gets her, won't he make the 'ringer' go!

Chorus:
Click go the shears boys, click, click, click;
Wide is his blow and his hands move quick,
The ringer looks round and is beaten by a blow,
And curses the old snagger with the bare-bellied yeo.

In the middle of the floor, in his cane-bottomed chair
Is the boss of the board, with eyes everywhere;
Notes well each fleece as it comes to the screen,
Paying strict attention if it's taken off clean.

The colonial experience man, he is there, of course,
With his shiny leggin's, just got off his horse;
Casting round his eye, like a real connoisseur,
Whistling the old tune, 'I'm the Perfect Lure.'

The tar-boy is there, awaiting in demand,
With his blackened tar-pot, and his tarry hand,
Sees one old sheep with a cut upon its back,
Hears what he's waiting for, 'Tar here, Jack!'

Shearing is all over and we've all got our cheques.
Roll up your swag boys, we're off on the tracks;
The first pub we come to, it's there we'll have a spree,
And everyone that comes along, it's 'Have a drink with me!'

Down by the bar the old shearer stands,
Grasping his glass in his thin bony hands;
Fixed is his gaze on a green-painted keg,
Glory, he'll get down on it, ere he stirs a peg.

There we leave him standing, shouting for all hands,
Whilst all around him, every drinker stands:
His eyes are on the cask, which is now lowering fast,
He works hard, he drinks hard, and goes to hell at last!

The Spider by the Gwydir

By the sluggish River Gwydir
    Lived a wicked red-backed spider,
Who was just about as vicious as could be:
    And the place that he was camped in
    Was a rusty Jones's jam-tin
In a paddock by the show-grounds at Moree.

Near him lay a shearer snoozin':
    He had been on beer and boozin'
All through the night and all the previous day;
    And the rookin' of the rookers,
    And the noise of showtime spruikers,
Failed to wake him from the trance in which he lay.

Then a crafty-lookin' spieler
With a dainty little sheila
Came along collecting wood to make a fire.
Said the spieler, 'He's a boozer
And he's goin' to be a loser:
If he isn't, you can christen me a liar.

'Hustle round and keep nit honey,
While I fan the mug for money,
And we'll have some little luxuries for tea.'
She answered, 'Don't be silly:
You go back and boil the billy.
You can safely leave the mug to little me!'

So she circled ever nearer,
Till she reached the dopey shearer
With his pockets bulgin', fast asleep and snug:
But she did not see the spider
That was ringin' close beside her,
For her mind was on the money and the mug.

The spider sighted dinner.
He'd been daily growing thinner;
He'd been fasting and was hollow as an urn.
As she eyed the bulging pocket,
He just darted like a rocket
And he bit that rookin' sheila on the stern.

Then the sheila raced off squealin',
And her clothes she was un-peelin':
To hear her yells would make you feel forlorn.
One hand the bite was pressin',
While the other was undressin',
And she reached the camp the same as she was born!

Then the shearer, pale and haggard,
Woke, and back to town he staggered,
Where he caught the train and gave the booze a rest:

And he'll never know the spider,
That was camped beside the Gwydir,
Had saved him sixty smackers of the best!

Mad Jack's Cockatoo

There's a man that went out in the floodtime and drought,
  By the banks of the outer Barcoo,
And they called him Mad Jack 'cause the swag on his back
  Was the perch for an old cockatoo.

By the towns near and far, in sheds, shanty and bar
  Came the yarns of Mad Jack and his bird,
And this tale I relate (it was told by a mate)
  Is just one of the many I've heard.

Now Jack was a bloke who could drink, holy smoke,
  He could swig twenty mugs to my ten,
And that old cockatoo, it could sink quite a few,
  And it drank with the rest of the men.

One day when the heat was a thing hard to beat,
  Mad Jack and his old cockatoo
Came in from the West – at the old Swagman's Rest
  Jack ordered the schooners for two.

And when these had gone down he forked out half a crown,
  And they drank till the money was spent:
Then Jack pulled out a note from his old tattered coat
  And between them they drank every cent.

Then the old cockatoo, it swore red, black and blue,
  And it knocked all the mugs off the bar;
Then it flew through the air, and it pulled at the hair
  Of a bloke who was drinking Three Star.

And it jerked out the pegs from the barrels and kegs,
  Knocked the bottles all down from the shelf,
With a sound like a cheer it dived into the beer,
  And it finished up drowning itself.

When at last Mad Jack woke from his sleep he ne'er spoke,
  But he cried like a lost husband's wife,
And each quick falling tear made a flood with the beer,
  And the men had to swim for their life.

Then Mad Jack he did drown; when the waters went down
  He was lying there stiffened and blue,
And it's told far and wide that stretched out by his side
  Was his track-mate – the old cockatoo.

Bluey Brink

There once was a shearer, by name Bluey Brink,
A devil for work and a devil for drink;
He could shear his two hundred a day without fear,
And drink without winking four gallons of beer.

Now Jimmy the barman who served out the drink,
He hated the sight of this here Bluey Brink,
Who stayed much too late, and who came much too soon,
At evening, at morning, at night and at noon.

One morning as Jimmy was cleaning the bar,
With sulphuric acid he kept in a jar,
Old Bluey come yelling and bawling with thirst:
'Whatever you've got Jim, just hand me the first!'

Now it ain't in the histories, it ain't put in print,
But Bluey drank acid with never a stint,
Saying, 'That's the stuff, Jimmy! Well, strike me stone dead,
This'll make me the ringer of Stevenson's shed!'

Now all that long day as he served out the beer,
Poor Jimmy was sick with his trouble and fear;
Too worried to argue, too anxious to fight,
Seeing the shearer a corpse in his fright.

When early next morning, he opened the door,
Then along came the shearer, asking for more,
With his eyebrows all singed and his whiskers deranged,
And holes in his hide like a dog with the mange.

Says Jimmy, 'And how did you find the new stuff?'
Says Bluey, 'It's fine, but I've not had enough!
It gives me great courage to shear and to fight,
But why does that stuff set my whiskers alight?

'I thought I knew drink, but I must have been wrong,
For what you just give me was proper and strong;
It set me to coughing and you know I'm no liar,
And every cough set my whiskers on fire!'

One of the Has-beens

I'm one of the has-beens, a shearer I mean;
I once was a ringer and used to shear clean;
I could make the wool roll off like the soil from the plough,
But you may not believe me, because I can't do it now.

Chorus:
I'm as awkward as a new chum, and I'm used to the frown,
That the boss often shows me, saying, 'Keep them blades
down!'

I've shore with Pat Hogan, Bill Bright and Jack Gunn,
Charlie Fergus, Tommy Layton and the great roaring
Dunn;
They brought from the Lachlan the best they could find,
But not one among 'em could leave me behind.

Well, it's no use complaining, I'll never say die,
Though the days of fast shearing for me have gone by;
I'll take the world easy, shear slowly and clean,
And I merely have told you just what I have been.

How the Sailor Rode the Brumby

There was an agile sailor lad
Who longed to know the bush:
So with his swag and billy-can
He said he'd make a push.
He left his ship in Moreton Bay
And faced the Western run,
And asked his way, ten times a day,
And steered for Bandy's Run.

Said Bandy: 'You can start, my son,
If you can ride ride a horse;'
For stockmen on the cattle-run
Were wanted there, of course.
Now Jack had strode the cross-bars oft
On many a bounding sea,
So reckoned he'd be safe enough
On any moke you see.

They caught him one and saddled it,
And led it from the yard:
It champed a bit and sidled round
And at the sailor sparred.
Jack towed her to him with a grin,
He eyed her fore and aft;
Then thrust his foot the gangway in
And swung aboard the craft.

The watchers tumbled off the rail;
The boss lay down and roared,
While Jack held tight by mane and tail
And rocked about on board.

But still he clung as monkeys cling
To rudder, line and flap,
Although at every bound and spring
They thought his neck must snap.

They stared to see him stick aloft
– The brum. bucked fierce and free,
But he had strode the cross-bars oft
On many a rolling sea.
The saddle from the rolling back
Went spinning in mid-air,
Whilst two big boots were flung off Jack
And four shoes off the mare.

The bridle broke and left her free –
He grasped her round the neck;
'We're 'mong the breakers now,' cried he,
'There's bound to be a wreck.'
The brumby struck and snorted loud,
She reared and pawed the air;
It was the grandest sight the crowd
Had ever witnessed there.

For Jack with arms and legs held tight
The brumby's neck hung round
And yelled, 'A pilot, quick as light,
Or strike me I'm aground.'
The whites and blacks climbed on the rails,
The boss stood smiling by
As Jack exclaimed, 'Away she sails!'
– The brum. began to fly.

She bounded first against the gate,
And Jack cried out, 'Astern!'
Then struck a whirlpool – at any rate
That was the sailor's yarn.

The brumby spun him round and round,
She reared and kicked and struck,
And with alternate bump and bound
In earnest began to buck.

A tree loomed on the starboard bow,
And 'Port your helm!' cried he;
She fouled a bush and he roared 'You scow!'
And 'Keep to the open sea!'
From ears to tail he rode her hard,
From tail to ears again,
One mile beyond the cattle-yard
And back across the plain.

Now high upon the pommel bumped,
Now clinging on the side,
And on behind the saddle lumped
With arms and legs flung wide.
They only laughed the louder then
When the mare began to back,
Until she struck the fence at last,
Then sat and looked at Jack.

He gasped, 'I'm safe in port at last,
I'll quit your bounding mane!'
Dropped off and sang, 'All danger's passed
And Jack's come home again.'
Old Jack has been a stockman now
On Bandy's Run for years,
Yet memories of that morning's fun
To many still bring tears.

The Maranoa Drovers

The night is dark and stormy, and the sky is clouded o'er;
  We'll saddle up our horses and away,
And we'll yard the squatter's cattle in the darkness of the night,
  And we'll keep them on the camp till break of day.

Chorus:

For we're going, going, going to Gunnedah so far,
  And we'll soon be into sunny New South Wales;
We'll bid farewell to Queensland, with its swampy coolibah –
  Happy drovers from the sandy Maranoa.

When the fires are burning bright through the darkness of the
      night,
  And the cattle camping quiet, well, I'm sure
That I wish for two o'clock when I call the other watch –
  This is droving from the sandy Maranoa.

Our beds made on the ground, we are sleeping all so sound
  When we're wakened by the distant thunder's roar,
And the lightning's vivid flash, followed by an awful crash –
  It's tough on drovers from the Maranoa.

We are up at break of day, and we're all soon on the way,
  For we always have to go ten miles or more;
It don't do to loaf about, or the squatter will come out –
  He's strict on drovers from the Maranoa.

Oh we'll soon be on the Moonbi and we'll cross the Barwon
      too:
  Then we'll be out on the rolling plains once more;
And we'll shout hurrah for Queensland and its swampy
      coolibah,
  And the cattle that came off the Maranoa!

The Flash Stockman

I'm a stockman to my trade, and they call me ugly Dave;
I'm old and grey and only got one eye.
In a yard I'm good, of course, but just put me on a horse,
And I'll go where lots of young 'uns daren't try.

I lead 'em through the gidgee over country rough and ridgy.
I lose 'em in the very worst of scrub;
I can ride both rough and easy, with a dewdrop I'm a daisy,
And a right-down bobby-dazzler in a pub.

Just watch me use a whip, I can give the dawdlers gyp,
I can make the bloody echoes roar and ring;
With a branding-iron, well, I'm a perfect flaming swell,
In fact, I'm duke of every blasted thing.

To watch me skin a sheep, it's so lovely you could weep;
I can act the silvertail as if my blood was blue;
You can strike me pink or dead, if I stood upon my head,
I'd be just as good as any other two.

I've a notion in my pate, that it's luck, it isn't fate,
That I'm so far above the common run;
So in every thing I do, you could cut me fair in two,
For I'm much too bloody good to be in one!

A Thousand Mile Away

Hurrah for the old stock saddle, hurrah for the stock whip too,
Hurrah for the baldy pony, boys, to carry me westward ho;
To carry me westward ho, my boys, that's where the cattle stray,
On the far Barcoo where they eat nardoo, a thousand mile
   away.

Then give your horses rein, across the open plain;
We'll crack our whips like a thunderbolt, nor care what some
   folk say;
And a-running we'll bring home them cattle that now roam
On the far Barcoo and the Flinders too, a thousand mile away.

Knee deep in grass we've got to pass, the truth I'm bound to
   tell,
Where in three weeks the cattle get as fat as they can swell;
As fat as they can swell, my boys, a thousand pound they weigh,
On the far Barcoo and the Flinders too, a thousand mile away.

No Yankee hide e'er grew outside such beef as we can freeze;
No Yankee pastures feed such steers as we send o'er the seas –
As we send o'er the seas, my boys, in shipments every day,
From the far Barcoo where they eat nardoo, a thousand mile
away.

So put me up with a snaffle, and a four or five inch spur,
And fourteen foot of greenhide whip to chop their flaming fur;
I'll yard them snuffy cattle in a way that's safe to swear,
I'll make them Queensland cattlemen sit back in the saddle
and stare.

Hurrah for the old stock saddle, hurrah for the stock whip too,
Hurrah for the baldy pony, boys, to carry me westward ho;
To carry me westward ho, my boys, that's where the cattle
stray,
On the far Barcoo where they eat nardoo, a thousand mile
away.

Bullocky Bill

As I came down Talbingo Hill
   I heard a maiden cry,
'There goes old Bill the Bullocky,
   He's bound for Gundagai
A better poor old beggar
   Never cracked an honest crust,
A tougher poor old beggar,
   Never drug a whip through dust.'
His team got bogged on the Five Mile Creek.
   Bill lashed and swore and cried,
'If Nobby don't get me out of this,
   I'll tattoo his bloody hide;'
But Nobby strained and broke his yoke,
   Poked out the leader's eye,
And the dog sat – in the tucker-box,
   Five miles from Gundagai!

Five Miles from Gundagai

I'm used to punchin' bullock-teams
  Across the hills and plains,
I've teamed outback this forty years
  In blazin' droughts and rains,
I've lived a heap of trouble down
  Without a bloomin' lie,
But I can't forget what happened me
  Five miles from Gundagai.

'Twas gettin' dark, the team got bogged,
  The axle snapped in two;
I lost me matches an' me pipe,
  So what was I to do?
The rain came on, 'twas bitter cold,
  And hungry too was I,
And the dog he sat in the tucker-box,
  Five miles from Gundagai.

Some blokes I know has stacks o' luck,
  No matter 'ow they fall,
But there was I, Lord love a duck!
  No blasted luck at all.
I couldn't make a pot 'o tea,
  Nor get me trousers dry,
And the dog sat in the tucker-box,
  Five miles from Gundagai.

I can forgive the blinkin' team,
  I can forgive the rain,
I can forgive the dark and cold,
  And go through it again,
I can forgive me rotten luck,
  But hang me till I die,
I can't forgive that bloody dog
  Five miles from Gundagai.

Holy Dan

It was in the Queensland drought;
  And over hill and dell,
No grass – the water far apart,
  All dry and hot as hell.
The wretched bullock teams drew up
  Beside a water-hole –
They'd struggled on through dust and drought
  For days to reach this goal.

And though the water rendered forth
  A rank, unholy stench,
The bullocks and the bullockies
  Drank deep their thirst to quench.

Two of the drivers cursed and swore
  As only drivers can.
The other one, named Daniel,
  Best known as Holy Dan,
Admonished them and said it was
  The Lord's all-wise decree;
And if they'd only watch and wait,
  A change they'd quickly see.

'Twas strange that of Dan's bullocks
  Not one had gone aloft;
But this, he said, was due to prayer
  And supplication oft.
At last one died but Dan was calm,
  He hardly seemed to care;
He knelt beside the bullock's corpse
  And offered up a prayer.

'One bullock Thou has taken, Lord,
  And so it seemeth best.
Thy will be done, but see my need
  And spare to me the rest!'

A month went by. Dan's bullocks now
    Were dying every day,
But still on each occasion would
    The faithful fellow pray,
'Another Thou hast taken, Lord,
    And so it seemeth best.
Thy will be done, but see my need,
    And spare to me the rest!'

And still they camped beside the hole,
    And still it never rained,
And still Dan's bullocks died and died,
    Till only one remained.
Then Dan broke down – good Holy Dan –
    The man who never swore.
He knelt beside the latest corpse,
    And here's the prayer he prore.

'That's nineteen Thou has taken, Lord,
    And now You'll plainly see
You'd better take the bloody lot:
    One's no damn good to me!'
The other drivers laughed so much
    They shook the sky around;
The lightning flashed, the thunder roared,
    And Holy Dan was drowned.

Wallaby Stew

Poor Dad, he got five years or more, as everybody knows,
And now he lives in Maitland gaol, broad arrows on his
    clothes;
He branded old Brown's cleanskins and he never left a tail
So I'll relate the family's fate since Dad got put in gaol.

Chorus:
So stir the wallaby stew, make soup of the kangaroo tail;
I tell you things is pretty tough since Dad got put in gaol.

Our sheep all died a month ago, of footrot and the fluke;
Our cow got shot last Christmas day by my big brother Luke
Our mother's got a shearer cove forever within hail;
The family will have grown a bit when Dad gets out of gaol.

Our Bess got shook upon some bloke, but he's gone, we don't
    know where;
He used to act about the sheds, but he ain't acted square;
I sold the buggy on my own, and the place is up for sale;
That won't be all that has been junked when Dad comes out
    of gaol.

They let Dad out before his time to give us a surprise.
He came and slowly looked around, then gently blessed our
    eyes;
He shook hands with the shearer cove, and said that things
    seemed stale,
And left him here to shepherd us, and battled back into gaol.

McQuade's Curse

May Satan, with a rusty crook,
Catch every goat in Tallarook;
May Mrs Melton's latest spook
Haunt all old maids in Tallarook;
May China's oldest pig-tailed cook
Spoil chops and steaks in Tallarook;
May all the frogs in Doogalook
Sing every night in Tallarook;
May Reedy Creek create a brook
To swamp the flats in Tallarook;
May rabbits ever find a nook
To breed apace in Tallarook;
May Sin Ye Sun and Sam Ah Fook
Steal all the fowls in Tallarook;
May Ikey Moses make a book
To stiffen sport in Tallarook;

May sirens fair as Lalla Rook
Tempt all old men in Tallarook;
May every paddock yield a stook
Of smutty wheat in Tallarook;
May good St Peter overlook
The good deeds done in Tallarook;
May each Don Juan who forsook
His sweetheart live in Tallarook;
May all who Matthew's pledges took
Get rolling drunk in Tallarook;
May every pigeon breed a rook
To spoil the crops in Tallarook;
May I get ague, gout and fluke
If I drink rum in Tallarook.

VI

(1885-1914)

LITERARY BUSH BALLADS

THIS was the period when a romantic patriotic sentiment played its part in bringing the Australian nation into being. Most patriots at the time felt that specifically or characteristically Australian values were to be seen most clearly in the bush; because bush life, necessarily, differed most markedly from what was still felt to be the norm – life in Britain. Hence this was the great period of the bush ballad, which both reflected and helped to inspire nationalist sentiments.

The verses grouped in this section are termed 'literary' only as a short-hand means of distinguishing them from the anonymous folk-verse exemplified in Section V. Most of these 'literary' balladists had considerable direct experience of bush life and their work is frankly popular and unsophisticated, owing little to the scholar's lamp or to the refined susceptibilities of the aesthete. Many latter-day critics have damned these bush ballads for their very virtues – directness, raciness, and popularity: but a good stockhorse is not, and perhaps should not aspire to be, a thoroughbred.

HENRY LAWSON (1867-1922)

Son of Peter Larsen, a Norwegian seaman who deserted ship to dig for gold, and his wife (*neé* Louisa Albury), Henry Lawson, as he later called himself, was born in a tent on the Grenfell gold-fields (N.S.W.). His parents took up a selection at Pipeclay, later known as Eurunderee, near Mudgee, and Lawson spent his boyhood on this poor bush farm. Most of his adult life was spent in Sydney, though he made two trips to Western Australia, one to New Zealand, and one to England. Most of his work, however, was inspired by his boyhood experience of bush life and by a six months' sojourn in the outback during 1892.

It is generally agreed that his short stories reach a far higher literary level than his poems. Often dismissed as mere jingles, the latter have nevertheless remained extremely popular because they express so directly the common man's attitude to his life and his fellows. Perhaps it would be more accurate to say the attitude widely admired if not always as widely practised, by the Australian common man. Some of Lawson's verses, like *The Captain of the Push* became so popular as to have passed into folk circulation in innumerable versions. In fact it will probably never be certainly known whether the anonymous and indelicate verses circulating orally in Australia and known as *The Bastard from the Bush,* inspired Lawson's poem or whether the reverse happened.

Bill

He shall live to the end of this mad old world as he's lived
    since the world began;
He never has done any good for himself, but was good to
    every man.
He never has done any good for himself, and I'm sure that
    he never will;
He drinks, and he swears, and he fights at times, and his name
    is mostly Bill.

He carried a freezing mate to his cave, and nursed him, for all
    I know,
When Europe was mainly a sheet of ice, thousands of years ago.
He has stuck to many a mate since then, he is with us every-
    where still –
He loves and gambles when he is young, and the girls stick up
    for Bill.

He has rowed to a wreck, when the lifeboat failed, with Jim
    in a crazy boat;
He has given his lifebelt many a time, and sunk that another
    might float.

He has 'stood 'em off' while others escaped, when the niggers
    rushed from the hill,
And rescue parties that came too late have found what was left
    of Bill.

He has thirsted on deserts that others might drink, he has given
    lest others should lack,
He has staggered half-blinded through fire or drought with a
    sick man on his back.
He is first to the rescue in tunnel or shaft, from Bulli to Broken
    Hill,
When the water breaks in or the fire breaks out, a leader of
    men is Bill!

He wears no Humane Society's badge for the fearful deaths
    he braved;
He seems ashamed of the good he did, and ashamed of the
    lives he saved.
If you chance to know of a noble deed he has done, you had
    best keep still;
If you chance to know of a kindly act, you mustn't let on to
    Bill.

He is fierce at a wrong, he is firm in right, he is kind to the
    weak and mild;
He will slave all day and sit up all night by the side of a
    neighbour's child.
For a woman in trouble he'd lay down his life, nor think as
    another man will;
He's a man all through, and no other man's wife has ever
    been worse for Bill.

He is good for the noblest sacrifice, he can do what few men
    can:
He will break his heart that the girl he loves may marry a
    better man.

There's many a mother and wife tonight whose heart and
eyes will fill
When she thinks of the days of the long-ago when she might
have stuck to Bill.

Maybe he's in trouble or hard up now, and travelling far for
work,
Or fighting a dead past down tonight in a lone camp west of
Bourke.
When he's happy and flush, take your sorrow to him and
borrow as much as you will:
But when he's in trouble or stony-broke, you never will hear
from Bill.

And when, because of its million sins, this earth is cracked like
a shell,
He will stand by a mate at the Judgment Seat and comfort
him down in – Well, –
I haven't much sentiment left to waste, but let cynics sneer as
they will,
Perhaps God will fix up the world again for the sake of the
likes of Bill.

Shearers

No church-bell rings them from the Track,
   No pulpit lights their blindness –
'Tis hardship, drought, and homelessness
   That teach those Bushmen kindness:
The mateship born, in barren lands,
   Of toil and thirst and danger,
The camp-fare for the wanderer set,
   The first place to the stranger.

They do the best they can today –
   Take no thought of the morrow;
Their way is not the old-world way –
   They live to lend and borrow.

When shearing's done and cheques gone wrong,
   They call it 'time to slither!' –
They saddle up and say 'so-long!'
   And ride the Lord knows whither.

And though he may be brown or black,
   Or wrong man there, or right man,
The mate that's steadfast to his mates
   They call that man a 'white man!'
They tramp in mateship side by side –
   The Protestant and Roman –
They call no biped lord or sir,
   And touch their hat to no man!

They carry in their swags, perhaps,
   A portrait and a letter –
And, maybe, deep down in their hearts,
   The hope of 'something better.'
Where lonely miles are long to ride,
   And long, hot days recurrent,
There's lots of time to think of men
   They might have been – but weren't.

They turn their faces to the west
   And leave the world behind them
(Their drought-dry graves are seldom set
   Where even mates can find them).
They know too little of the world
   To rise to wealth or greatness:
But in these lines I gladly pay
   My tribute to their straightness.

Ballad of the Drover

Across the stony ridges,
   Across the rolling plain,
Young Harry Dale, the drover,
   Comes riding home again.

And well his stock-horse bears him,
  And light of heart is he,
And stoutly his old packhorse
  Is trotting by his knee.

Up Queensland way with cattle
  He's travelled regions vast,
And many months have vanished
  Since home-folks saw him last.
He hums a song of someone
  He hopes to marry soon;
And hobble-chains and camp-ware
  Keep jingling to the tune.

Beyond the hazy dado
  Against the lower skies
And yon blue line of ranges
  The station homestead lies.
And thitherward the drover
  Jogs through the lazy noon
While hobble-chains and camp-ware
  Are jingling to a tune.

An hour has filled the heavens
  With storm-clouds inky black;
At times the lightning trickles
  Around the drover's track;
But Harry pushes onward,
  His horses' strength he tries,
In hope to reach the river
  Before the flood shall rise.

The thunder, pealing o'er him,
  Goes rumbling down the plain;
And sweet on thirsty pastures
  Beats fast the plashing rain;

Then every creek and gully
  Sends forth its tribute flood –
The river runs a banker,
  All stained with yellow mud.

Now Harry speaks to Rover,
  The best dog on the plains,
And to his hardy horses,
  And strokes their shaggy manes:
'We've breasted bigger rivers
  When floods were at their height,
Nor shall this gutter stop us
  From getting home tonight!'

The thunder growls a warning
  The blue, forked lightnings gleam;
The drover turns his horses
  To swim the fatal stream.
But, oh! the flood runs stronger
  Than e'er it ran before;
The saddle-horse is failing,
  And only half-way o'er!

When flashes next the lightning,
  The flood's grey breast is blank;
A cattle-dog and packhorse
  Are struggling up the bank.
But in the lonely homestead
  The girl shall wait in vain –
He'll never pass the stations
  In charge of stock again.

The faithful dog a moment
  Lies panting on the bank,
Then plunges through the current
  To where his master sank.
And round and round in circles
  He fights with failing strength,
Till, gripped by wilder waters,
  He fails and sinks at length.

Across the flooded lowlands
    And slopes of sodden loam
The packhorse struggles bravely
    To take dumb tidings home;
And mud-stained, wet, and weary,
    He goes by rock and tree,
With clanging chains and tinware
    All sounding eerily.

The Ballad of Mabel Clare
An Australian story to be read and sung hereafter

Ye children of the Land of Gold
    I sing a song to you,
And if the jokes are somewhat old,
    The main idea is new.
So, be it sung, by hut and tent,
    Where tall the native grows;
And understand, the song is meant
    For singing thro' the nose.

There dwelt a sound old cockatoo
    On western hills far out –
Where ev'rything is green and blue,
    Except, of course, in drought –
A crimson Anarchist was he,
    Held other men in scorn,
Yet preach'd that ev'ry man was free,
    And also 'ekal born.'

He lived in his ancestral hut –
    His missus was not there –
And there was no one with him but
    His daughter, Mabel Clare.
Her eyes and hair were like the sun;
    Her foot was like a mat;
Her cheeks a trifle overdone;
    She was a democrat.

144

A manly independence born
   Among the trees she had,
She treated womankind with scorn,
   And often cursed her dad.
She hated swells and shining lights,
   For she had seen a few,
And she believed in 'women's rights'
   (She mostly got 'em, too).

A stranger at the neighb'ring run
   Sojourned, the squatter's guest,
He was unknown to anyone,
   But like a swell was dress'd;
He had an eyeglass to his eye,
   A collar to his ears,
His feet were made to tread the sky.
   His mouth was formed for sneers.

He wore the latest toggerie,
   The loudest thing in ties –
'Twas generally reckoned he
   Was something in disguise.
But who he was, or whence he came,
   Was long unknown, except,
Unto the squatter, who the name
   A noble secret kept.

And strolling in the noontide heat,
   Beneath the 'blinding glare,'
This noble stranger chanced to meet
   The radiant Mabel Clare.
She saw at once he was a swell –
   According to her lights –
But, ah! 'tis very sad to tell,
   She met him oft of nights.

And, strolling through a moonlit gorge,
   She chatted all the while
Of Ingersoll, and Henry George,
   And Bradlaugh and Carlyle –

In short, he learned to love the girl,
   And things went on like this,
Until he said he was an Earl,
   And asked her to be his.

'Oh, say no more, Lord Kawlinee,
   Oh, say no more!' she said;
'Oh, say no more, Lord Kawlinee,
   I wish that I was dead:
My head is in a hawful whirl,
   The truth I dare not tell –
I am a democratic girl
   And cannot wed a swell!'

'Oh, love!' he cried, 'but you forget
   That you are most unjust;
'Twas not my fault that I was set
   Within the uppercrust.
Heed not the yarns the poets tell –
   Oh, darling, do not doubt
A simple lord can love as well
   As any rouseabout!

'For you I'll give my fortune up,
   I'll go to work for you:
I'll put the money in the cup
   And drop the title, too.
Oh, fly with me! Oh, fly with me!
   Across the mountains blue –
Hoh, fly with me! *Oh, fly with me*!' –
   That very night she flew.

They took the train and journeyed down –
   Across the range they sped –
Until they came to Sydney town,
   Where shortly they were wed.

And still upon the western wild
   Admiring teamsters tell
How Mabel's father cursed his child
   For clearing with a swell.

'What ails my bird this bridal night,'
   Exclaimed Lord Kawlinee;
'What ails my own this bridal night –
   Oh, love, confide in me!'
'Oh now,' she said, 'that I am yaws
   You'll let me weep – I must –
I did desert the people's cause
   To join the uppercrust.'

Oh proudly smiled his lordship then –
   His chimney-pot he floor'd –
'Look up, my love, and smile again,
   For I am not a lord!'
His eye glass from his eye he tore,
   The dickey from his breast,
And turned and stood his bride before
   A rouseabout – confess'd!

'Unknown I've loved you long,' he said,
   And I have loved you true –
A-shearing in your guvner's shed
   I learned to worship you.
I do not care for place or pelf,
   For now, my love, I'm sure
That you will love me for myself
   And not because I'm poor.

'To prove your love I spent my cheque
   To buy this swell rig-out;
So fling your arms about my neck
   For I'm a rouseabout!'

At first she gave a startled cry,
  Then, safe from care's alarms,
She sigh'd a soul-subduing sigh
  And sank into his arms.

He pawned the togs and home he took
  His bride in all her charms;
The proud old cockatoo received
  The pair with open arms.
And long they lived, the faithful bride,
  The noble rouseabout –
And if she wasn't satisfied
  She never let it out.

To My Cultured Critics

Fight through ignorance, want, and care –
  Through the griefs that crush the spirit;
Push your way to a fortune fair,
  And the smiles of the world you'll merit.
Long, as a boy, for the chance to learn –
  For the chance that Fate denies you;
Win degrees where the Life-lights burn,
  And scores will teach and advise you.

My cultured friends! you have come too late
  With your bypath nicely graded;
I've fought thus far on my track of Fate,
  And I'll follow the rest unaided.
Must I be stopped by a college gate
  On the track of Life encroaching?
Be dumb to Love, and be dumb to Hate,
  For the lack of a pedant's coaching?

You grope for Truth in a language dead –
  In the dust 'neath tower and steeple!
What do you know of the tracks we tread,
  And what of the living people?

I '*must* read this, and that, and the rest,'
    And write as the cult expects me? –
I'll read the book that may please me best,
    And write as my heart directs me!

You were quick to pick on a faulty line
    That I strove to put my soul in:
Your eyes were keen for a dash of mine
    In the place of a semi-colon –
And blind to the rest. And is it for such
    As you I must brook restriction?
'I was taught too little?' I learnt too much
    To care for a scholar's diction!

Must I turn aside from my destined way
    For a task your Joss would find me?
I come with strength of the living day,
    And with half the world behind me;
I leave you alone in your cultured halls
    To drivel and croak and cavil:
Till your voice goes farther than college walls,
    Keep out of the tracks we travel!

A Word to Texas Jack

Texas Jack, you are amusin'. Great Lord Harry how I laughed
When I seen your rig and saddle with its bulwarks fore-and-aft;
Holy smoke! From such a saddle how the dickens can you fall?
Why, I've seen a gal ride bareback with no bridle on at all!

Gosh! so help me! strike me balmy! if a bit o' scenery
Like of you in all your rig-out on this earth I ever see!
How I'd like to see a bushman use your fixings, Texas Jack –
On the remnant of a saddle he could ride to hell and back.
Why, I've heerd a mother cheerin' when her kid went tossin'
    by,
Ridin' bareback on a bucker that had murder in his eye.

What? you've come to learn the natives how to sit a horse's
    back!
Learn the bloomin' cornstalk ridin'? W'at yer giv'n us,
    Texas Jack?
Learn the cornstalk! Flamin' jumptup! now where has my
    country gone?
Why, the cornstalk's mother often rides the day afore he's
    born!

You may talk about your ridin' in the city, bold an' free,
Talk o' ridin' in the city, Texas Jack; but where'd you be
When the stock-horse snorts an' bunches all 'is quarters in a
    hump,
And the saddle climbs a sapling, an' the horseshoes split a
    stump?
No, before you teach the native you must ride without a fall
Up a gum, or down a gully, nigh as steep as any wall –
You must swim the roarin' Darlin' when the flood is at its
    height
Bearin' down the stock an' stations to the great Australian
    Bight.

You can't count the bulls an' bisons that you copped with
    your lassoo –
But a stout old myall bullock p'raps ud learn you somethin'
    new;
You had better make your will an' leave your papers neat an'
    trim
Before you make arrangements for the lassooin' of *him*;
Ere your horse and you is cat's-meat – fittin' fate for sich
    galoots –
And your saddle's turned to laces like we put in blucher boots.

And you say you're death on Injins! We've got somethin' in
    your line –
If you think your fightin's ekal to the likes of Tommy Ryan.
Take your carcass up to Queensland where the alligators chew
And the carpet-snake is handy with his tail for a lassoo;

Ride across the hazy regions where the lonely emus wail
An' you'll find the black'll track you while you're lookin' for
  his trail;
He can track you without stoppin' for a thousand miles or
  more –
Come again, and he will show you where you spit the year
  before.
But you'd best be mighty careful – you'll be sorry you kem here
When you're skewered to the fakements of your saddle with
  a spear;
When the boomerang is sailin' in the air, then Heaven help
  you.
It will cut your head off goin', an' come back again to scalp you.

*

P.S. – As poet and as Yankee I will greet you, Texas Jack,
For it isn't no ill-feelin' that is gettin' up my back;
But I won't see this land crowded by each Yank and British
  cuss
Who takes it in his head to come a-civilizin' us.
Though on your own great continent there's misery in the
  towns
An' not a few untitled lords, and kings without their crowns,
I will admit your countrymen is busted big, an' free,
An' great on ekal rites of men and great on liberty;
I will admit your fathers punched the gory tyrant's head –
But then we've got our heroes, too, the diggers that is dead,
The plucky men of Ballarat, who toed the scratch so well,
And broke the nose of Tyranny and made his peepers swell,
For yankin' Lib.'s gold tresses in the roarin' days gone by,
An' doublin' up his dirty fist to black her bonny eye;
So when it comes to ridin' mokes, or hoistin' out the Chow,
Or stickin' up for labour's rights, we don't want showin' how.
They came to learn us cricket in the days of long ago,
An' Hanlan came from Canada to learn us how to row,
An' 'doctors' come from Frisco just to learn us how to skite,
An' pugs from all the lands on earth to learn us how to fight;
An' when they go, as like as not, we find we're taken in,
They've left behind no learnin' – but they've carried off our tin.

The Captain of the Push

As the night was falling slowly down on city, town, and bush,
From a slum in Jones's Alley sloped the Captain of the Push;
And he scowled towards the North, and he scowled towards
  the South,
As he hooked his little fingers in the corners of his mouth.
Then his whistle, loud and piercing, woke the echoes of 'The
  Rocks,'
And a dozen ghouls came sloping round the corners of the
  blocks.

There was nought to rouse their anger; yet the oath that each
  one swore
Seemed less fit for publication than the one that went before.
For they spoke the gutter language with the easy flow that
  comes
Only to the men whose childhood knew the gutters and the
  slums.
Then they spat in turn, and halted; and the one that came
  behind,
Spitting fiercely at the pavement, called on Heaven to strike
  him blind.

Let me first describe the captain, bottle-shouldered, pale and
  thin:
He was just the beau-ideal of a Sydney larrikin.
E'en his hat was most suggestive of the place where Pushes live
With a gallows-tilt that no one, save a larrikin, can give;
And the coat, a little shorter than the fashion might require,
Showed a (more or less uncertain) lower part of his attire.

That which tailors know as 'trousers' – known to him as
  'blooming bags' –
Hanging loosely from his person, swept, with tattered ends,
  the flags;
And he had a pointed sternpost to the boots that peeped below
(Which he laced up from the centre of the nail of his great toe).

And he wore his shirt uncollared, and the tie correctly wrong;
But I think his vest was shorter than should be on one so long.

Then the captain crooked his finger at a stranger on the kerb,
Whom he qualified politely with an adjective and verb,
And he begged the Gory Bleeders that they wouldn't interrupt
Till he gave an introduction – it was painfully abrupt –
'Here's the bleedin' push, my covey – here's a (something)
    from the bush!
Strike me dead, he wants to join us!' said the captain of the
    push.

Said the stranger: 'I am nothing but a bushy and a dunce;
But I read about the Bleeders in the *Weekly Gasbag* once:
Sitting lonely in the humpy when the wind began to whoosh.
How I longed to share the dangers and the pleasures of the
    push!
Gosh! I hate the swells and good uns – I could burn 'em in
    their beds;
I am with you, if you'll have me, and I'll break their blazing
    heads.'

'Now, look here,' exclaimed the captain to the stranger from
    the bush,
'Now, look here – suppose a feller was to split upon the push,
Would you lay for him and down him, even if the traps were
    round?
Would you lay him out and kick him to a jelly on the ground?
Would you jump upon the nameless – kill, or cripple him, or
    both?
Speak? or else I'll – SPEAK!' The stranger answered, 'My
    kerlonial oath!'

'Now, look here,' exclaimed the captain to the stranger from
    the bush,
'Now, look here – suppose the Bleeders let you come and join
    the push,
Would you smash a bleedin' bobby if you got the blank alone?
Would you stoush a swell or Chinkie – split his garret with
    a stone?

Would you have a "moll" to keep you – like to swear off
    work for good?'
'Yes, my oath!' replied the stranger. 'My kerlonial oath!
    I would!'

'Now, look here,' exclaimed the captain to that stranger from
    the bush,
'Now, look here – before the Bleeders let you come and join
    the push.
You must prove that you're a blazer – you must prove that
    you have grit
Worthy of a Gory Bleeder – you must show your form a bit –
Take a rock and smash that winder!' and the stranger, nothing
    loth,
Took the rock and – smash! The Bleeders muttered 'My
    kerlonial oath!'

So they swore him in, and found him sure of aim and light
    of heel,
And his only fault, if any, lay in his excessive zeal.
He was good at throwing metal, but I chronicle with pain
That he jumped upon a victim, damaging the watch and chain
Ere the Bleeders had secured them; yet the captain of the push
Swore a dozen oaths in favour of the stranger from the bush.

Late next morn the captain, rising, hoarse and thirsty, from
    his lair,
Called the newly-feathered Bleeder; but the stranger wasn't
    there!
Quickly going through the pockets of his bloomin' bags he
    learned
That the stranger had been through them for the stuff his
    moll had earned;
And the language that he uttered I should scarcely like to tell
(Stars! and notes of exclamation! ! blank and dash will do
    as well).

That same night the captain's signal woke the echoes of The
    Rocks,
Brought the Gory Bleeders sloping through the shadows of
    the blocks;
And they swore the stranger's action was a blood-escaping
    shame,
While they waited for the nameless – but the nameless never
    came.
And the Bleeders soon forgot him; but the captain of the push
Still is laying round, in ballast, for the stranger 'from the bush.'

The Men Who Made Australia

(Written on the Occasion of the Royal Visit to Australia, 1901)

There'll be royal times in Sydney for the Cuff and Collar Push,
    There'll be lots of dreary drivel and clap-trap
From the men who own Australia, but who never knew the
    Bush,
    And who could not point their runs out on the map.
Oh, the daily Press will grovel as it never did before,
    There'll be many flags of welcome in the air,
And the Civil Service poet, he shall write odes by the score –
    But the men who made the land will not be there.

You shall meet the awful Lady of the latest Birthday Knight –
    (She is trying to be English, don't-cher-know?)
You shall hear the empty mouthing of the champion blather-
    skite,
    You shall hear the boss of local drapers blow.
There's be 'majahs' from the counter, tailors' dummies from
    the fleet,
    And to represent Australia here today,
There's the toady with his card-case and his cab in Downing
    Street;
    But the men who made Australia – where are they?

Call across the blazing sand wastes of the Never-Never Land!
   There are some who will not answer yet awhile,
Some whose bones rot in the mulga or lie bleaching on the
      sand,
   Died of thirst to win the land another mile.
Thrown from horses, ripped by cattle, lost on deserts: and
      the weak,
   Mad through loneliness or drink (no matter which),
Drowned in floods or dead of fever by the sluggish slimy creek –
   These are men who died to make the Wool-Kings rich.

*

There are carriages in waiting for the swells from over-sea,
   There are banquets in the latest London style,
While the men who made Australia live on damper, junk
      and tea –
   But the quiet voices whisper, 'Wait a while!'
For the sons of all Australia, they were born to conquer fate –
   And, where charity and friendship are sincere,
Where a sinner is a brother and a stranger is a mate,
   There the future of a nation's written clear.

Aye, the cities claim the triumphs of a land they do not know,
   But all empty is the day they celebrate!
For the men who made Australia federated long ago,
   And the men to rule Australia – they can wait.
Though the bed may be the rough bunk or the gum leaves
      or the sand,
   And the roof for half the year may be the sky –
There are men among the Bushmen who were born to save
      the land!
   And they'll take their places sternly by-and-by.

The Roaring Days

The night too quickly passes,
   And we are growing old,
So let us fill our glasses
   And toast the days of Gold!

When finds of wond'rous treasure,
   Set all the South ablaze.
And you and I were faithful mates,
   All through the roaring days.

When stately ships came sailing
   From every harbour's mouth,
And sought the Land of Promise
   That beckoned in the South;
Then southward streamed their streamers,
   And swelled their canvas full,
To speed the wildest dreamers
   E'er borne in vessel's hull.

Their shining Eldorado,
   Beneath the southern skies,
Was, day and night, for ever
   Before their shining eyes.
The brooding bush, awakened,
   Was stirred in wild unrest,
And all the year, a human stream
   Went pouring to the west.

The rough bush roads re-echoed
   The bar-room's noisy din,
When troops of stalwart horsemen
   Dismounted at the inn.
And oft the joyful greetings,
   And hearty clasp of hands,
Would tell of sudden meetings
   Of friends from other lands.

And when the cheery camp-fire
   Explored the bush with gleams,
The camping grounds were crowded
   With caravans of teams;

Then home the jests were driven,
    And good old songs were sung,
And choruses were given
    The strength of heart and lung.

Oft, when the camps were dreaming,
    And stars began to pale,
Through rugged ranges gleaming,
    Swept on the Royal Mail.
Behind five foaming horses,
    And lit by flashing lamps,
Old Cobb and Co., in royal state,
    Went dashing past the camps.

Oh! who would paint a goldfield,
    And limn the picture right,
As old Adventure saw it
    In early morning's light?
The yellow mounds of mullock,
    With spots of red and white,
The scattered quartz that glistened,
    Like diamonds in light.

The azure line of ridges,
    The bush of darkest green,
The little homes of calico,
    That dotted all the scene,
The flat, straw hats with ribands,
    That old engravings show –
The dress that still reminds us,
    Of sailors long ago.

I hear the fall of timber,
    From distant flats and fells,
The pealing of the anvils,
    As clear as little bells,
The rattle of the cradle,
    The clack of windlass boles,
The flutter of the crimson flags,
    Above the golden holes.

Ah! then their hearts were bolder,
  And if Dame Fortune frowned,
Their swags they'd lightly shoulder,
  And tramp to other ground.
Oh! they were lion-hearted,
  Who gave our country birth,
Stout sons of stoutest fathers born,
  From all the lands of earth.

Those golden days have vanished,
  And altered is the scene;
The diggings are deserted,
  The camping-grounds are green;
The flaunting flag of progress
  Is in the West unfurled,
The mighty bush with iron rails
  Is tethered to the world.

A. B. ('BANJO') PATERSON (1864-1941)

Born near Orange (N.S.W.) on a station which was owned and later managed by his father, Paterson was educated at Sydney Grammar School. He qualified as a solicitor but his adult life was divided between legal practice, journalism, and pastoral pursuits.

His bush ballads were, and are, quite as popular as Lawson's and some of them, such as *A Bushman's Song* and perhaps *Waltzing Matilda,* also passed into folk currency. His verses lack the note of class bitterness prominent in Lawson's work and, partly for this reason, present a more cheerful picture of bush life. Lawson's villains are usually wealthy or well-to-do people, whether squatters, or city employers. All bushmen – squatters, selectors, drovers, and swagmen alike – claim Paterson's regard, while he tends to see all city-dwellers as pusillanimous, second-class citizens.

Clancy of The Overflow

I had written him a letter which I had, for want of better
   Knowledge, sent to where I met him down the Lachlan,
     years ago;
He was shearing when I knew him, so I sent the letter to him,
   Just on spec, addressed as follows, 'Clancy, of The Overflow.'

And an answer came directed in a writing unexpected
   (And I think the same was written with a thumb-nail
     dipped in tar):
'Twas his shearing mate who wrote it, and *verbatim* I will
   quote it:
   'Clancy's gone to Queensland droving, and we don't know
    where he are.'

In my wild erratic fancy visions come to me of Clancy
   Gone a-droving 'down the Cooper' where the Western
    drovers go;

As the stock are slowly stringing, Clancy rides behind them
    singing,
    For the drover's life has pleasures that the townsfolk never
      know.

And the bush has friends to meet him, and their kindly voices
    greet him
    In the murmur of the breezes and the river on its bars,
And he sees the vision splendid of the sunlit plains extended,
    And at night the wondrous glory of the everlasting stars.

I am sitting in my dingy little office, where a stingy
    Ray of sunlight struggles feebly down between the houses
      tall,
And the foetid air and gritty of the dusty, dirty city,
    Through the open window floating, spreads its foulness
      over all.

And in place of lowing cattle, I can hear the fiendish rattle
    Of the tramways and the buses making hurry down the
      street;
And the language uninviting of the gutter children fighting
    Comes fitfully and faintly through the ceaseless tramp of
      feet.

And the hurrying people daunt me, and their pallid faces
    haunt me
    As they shoulder one another in their rush and nervous
      haste,
With their eager eyes and greedy, and their stunted forms and
    weedy,
    For townsfolk have no time to grow, they have no time to
      waste.

And I somehow rather fancy that I'd like to change with
    Clancy,
    Like to take a turn at droving where the seasons come
      and go,

While he faced the round eternal of the cash-book and the
    journal –
  But I doubt he'd suit the office, Clancy of The Overflow.

The Man from Snowy River

There was movement at the station, for the word had passed
    around
  That the colt from old *Regret* had got away,
And had joined the wild bush horses – he was worth a thousand
    pound,
  So all the cracks had gathered to the fray.
All the tried and noted riders from the stations near and far
  Had mustered at the homestead overnight,
For the bushmen love hard riding where the wild bush horses
    are,
  And the stock-horse snuffs the battle with delight.

There was Harrison, who made his pile when *Pardon* won the
    Cup,
  The old man with his hair as white as snow;
But few could ride beside him when his blood was fairly up –
  He would go wherever horse and man could go.
And Clancy of the Overflow came down to lend a hand,
  No better horseman ever held the reins;
For never horse could throw him while the saddle girths would
    stand –
  He learnt to ride while droving on the plains.

And one was there, a stripling on a small and weedy beast;
  He was something like a racehorse undersized,
With a touch of Timor pony – three parts thorough-bred at
    least –
  And such as are by mountain horsemen prized.
He was hard and tough and wiry – just the sort that won't
    say die –
  There was courage in his quick impatient tread;
And he bore the badge of gameness in his bright and fiery eye,
  And the proud and lofty carriage of his head.

But still so light and weedy, one would doubt his power to stay,
    And the old man said, 'That horse will never do
For a long and tiring gallop – lad, you'd better stop away;
    Those hills are far too rough for such as you.'
So he waited, sad and wistful – only Clancy stood his friend –
    'I think we ought to let him come,' he said;
'I warrant he'll be with us when he's wanted at the end,
    For both his horse and he are mountain bred.

'He hails from Snowy River, up by Kosciusko's side,
    Where the hills are twice as steep and twice as rough;
Where a horse's hoofs strike firelight from the flint stones
        every stride,
    The man that holds his own is good enough.
And the Snowy River riders on the mountains make their home,
    Where the river runs those giant hills between;
I have seen full many horsemen since I first commenced to
        roam,
    But nowhere yet such horsemen have I seen.'

So he went; they found the horses by the big mimosa clump;
    They raced away towards the mountain's brow,
And the old man gave his orders, 'Boys, go at them from the
        jump,
    No use to try for fancy riding now.
And, Clancy, you must wheel them, try and wheel them to the
        right.
    Ride boldly, lad, and never fear the spills,
For never yet was rider that could keep the mob in sight,
    If once they gain the shelter of those hills.'

So Clancy rode to wheel them – he was racing on the wing
    Where the best and boldest riders take their place,
And he raced his stock-horse past them, and he made the
        ranges ring
    With the stock-whip, as he met them face to face.

Then they halted for a moment, while he swung the dreaded
  lash,
  But they saw their well-loved mountain full in view,
And they charged beneath the stock-whip with a sharp and
  sudden dash,
  And off into the mountain scrub they flew.

Then fast the horsemen followed, where the gorges deep and
  black
  Resounded to the thunder of their tread,
And the stock-whip woke the echoes, and they fiercely ans-
  wered back
  From cliffs and crags that beetled overhead.
And upward, ever upward, the wild horses held their way,
  Where mountain ash and kurrajong grew wide;
And the old man muttered fiercely, 'We may bid the mob
  good-day,
  No man can hold them down the other side.'

When they reached the mountain's summit, even Clancy took
  a pull –
  It well might make the boldest hold their breath;
The wild hop scrub grew thickly, and the hidden ground was
  full
  Of wombat holes, and any slip was death.
But the man from Snowy River let the pony have his head,
  And swung his stock-whip round and gave a cheer,
And raced him down the mountain like a torrent down its bed,
  While the others stood and watched in very fear.

He sent the flint-stones flying, but the pony kept his feet,
  He cleared the fallen timber in his stride,
And the man from Snowy River never shifted in his seat –
  It was grand to see that mountain horseman ride.
Through the stringy barks and saplings, on the rough and
  broken ground,
  Down the hillside at a racing pace he went;
And he never drew the bridle till he landed safe and sound
  At the bottom of that terrible descent.

He was right among the horses as they climbed the further hill,
  And the watchers on the mountain, standing mute,
Saw him ply the stock-whip fiercely; he was right among them still,
  As he raced across the clearing in pursuit.
Then they lost him for a moment, where two mountain gullies met
  In the ranges – but a final glimpse reveals
On a dim and distant hillside the wild horses racing yet,
  With the man from Snowy River at their heels.

And he ran them single-handed till their sides were white
    with foam;
  He followed like a bloodhound on their track,
Till they halted, cowed and beaten; then he turned their heads
    for home,
  And alone and unassisted brought them back.
But his hardy mountain pony he could scarcely raise a trot,
  He was blood from hip to shoulder from the spur;
But his pluck was still undaunted, and his courage fiery hot,
  For never yet was mountain horse a cur.

And down by Kosciusko, where the pine-clad ridges raise
  Their torn and rugged battlements on high,
Where the air is clear as crystal, and the white stars fairly blaze
  At midnight in the cold and frosty sky,
And where around the Overflow the reed-beds sweep and sway
  To the breezes, and the rolling plains are wide,
The man from Snowy River is a household word today,
  And the stockmen tell the story of his ride.

Saltbush Bill

Now this is the law of the Overland that all in the West obey –
A man must cover with travelling sheep a six-mile stage a day;
But this is the law which the drovers make, right easily under-
    stood,

They travel their stage where the grass is bad, but they camp
    where the grass is good;
They camp, and they ravage the squatter's grass till never a
    blade remains;
Then they drift away as the white clouds drift on the edge of
    the saltbush plains;
From camp to camp and from run to run they battle it hand
    to hand
For a blade of grass and the right to pass on the track of the
    Overland.

For this is the law of the Great Stock Routes, 'tis written in
    white and black –
The man that goes with a travelling mob must keep to a half-
    mile track;
And the drovers keep to a half-mile track on the runs where
    the grass is dead,
But they spread their sheep on a well-grassed run till they go
    with a two-mile spread.
So the squatters hurry the drovers on from dawn till the fall
    of night,
And the squatters' dogs and the drovers' dogs get mixed in a
    deadly fight;
Yet the squatters' men, though they hunt the mob, are willing
    the peace to keep,
For the drovers learn how to use their hands when they go
    with the travelling sheep.

But this is the tale of a jackeroo that came from a foreign
    strand,
And the fight that he fought with Saltbush Bill, the King of
    the Overland.
Now Saltbush Bill was a drover tough, as ever the country
    knew,
He had fought his way on the Great Stock Routes from the
    sea to the big Barcoo;
He could tell when he came to a friendly run that gave him a
    chance to spread,

And he knew where the hungry owners were that hurried his
  sheep ahead;
He was drifting down in the 'Eighty drought with a mob that
  could scarcely creep –
When kangaroos by the thousands starve, it is rough on the
  travelling sheep.

And he camped one night at the crossing-place on the edge of
  the Wilga run;
'We must manage a feed for them here,' he said, 'or half of
  the mob are done!'
So he spread them out when they left the camp wherever they
  liked to go,
Till he grew aware of a jackeroo with a station-hand in tow;
And they set to work on the straggling sheep, and with many
  a stockwhip crack
They forced them in where the grass was dead in the space of
  the half-mile track;
And William prayed that the hand of Fate might suddenly
  strike him blue
But he'd get some grass for his starving sheep in the teeth of
  that jackeroo.

So he turned and he cursed the jackeroo, he cursed him alive
  or dead,
From the soles of his great unwieldy feet to the crown of his
  ugly head,
With an extra curse on the moke he rode and the cur at his
  heels that ran,
Till the jackeroo from his horse got down and went for the
  droving man;
With the station-hand for his picker-up, though the sheep ran
  loose the while,
They battled it out on the saltbush plain in the regular prize-
  ring style.
Now, the new-chum fought for his honour's sake and the
  pride of the English race,
But the drover fought for his daily bread with a smile on his
  bearded face –

So he shifted ground and he sparred for wind and he made it
    a lengthy mill,
And from time to time as his scouts came in they whispered
    to Saltbush Bill –
'We have spread the sheep with a two-mile spread, and the
    grass it is something grand,
You must stick to him, Bill, for another round for the pride of
    the Overland.'
The new-chum made it a rushing fight, though never a blow
    got home,
Till the sun rode high in the cloudless sky and glared on the
    brick-red loam,
Till the sheep drew in to the shelter-trees and settled them
    down to rest;
Then the drover said he would fight no more and gave his
    opponent best.

So the new-chum rode to the station straight, and he told
    them a story grand
Of the desperate fight that he fought that day with the King
    of the Overland.
And the tale went home to the Public Schools of the pluck of
    the English swell,
How the drover fought for his very life, but blood in the end
    must tell.
But the travelling sheep and the Wilga sheep were boxed on
    the Old Man Plain.
'Twas a full week's work ere they drafted out and hunted
    them off again;
With a week's good grass in their wretched hides, with a curse
    and a stockwhip crack,
They hunted them off on the road once more to starve on the
    half-mile track.

And Saltbush Bill, on the Overland, will many a time recite
How the best day's work that he ever did was the day that he
    lost the fight.

How Gilbert Died

There's never a stone at the sleeper's head,
　　There's never a fence beside;
And the wandering stock on the grave may tread
　　Unnoticed and undenied;
But the smallest child on the watershed
　　Can tell you how Gilbert died.

For he rode at dusk with his comrade Dunn
　　To the hut at the Stockman's Ford;
In the waning light of the sinking sun
　　They peered with a fierce accord.
They were outlaws both – and on each man's head
　　Was a thousand pounds reward.

They had taken toll of the country round,
　　And the troopers came behind
With a black that tracked like a human hound
　　In the scrub and the ranges blind:
He could run the trail where a white man's eye
　　No sign of a track could find.

He had hunted them out of the One Tree Hill
　　And over the Old Man Plain,
But they wheeled their tracks with a wild beast's skill,
　　And they made for the range again;
Then away to the hut where their grandsire dwelt
　　They rode with a loosened rein.

And their grandsire gave them a greeting bold:
　　'Come in and rest in peace,
No safer place does the country hold –
　　With the night pursuit must cease,
And we'll drink success to the roving boys,
　　And to hell with the black police.'

But they went to death when they entered there
　　In the hut at the Stockman's Ford,

For their grandsire's words were as false as fair –
    They were doomed to the hangman's cord.
He had sold them both to the black police
    For the sake of the big reward.

In the depth of night there are forms that glide
    As stealthy as serpents creep,
And around the hut where the outlaws hide
    They plant in the shadows deep,
And they wait till the first faint flush of dawn
    Shall waken their prey from sleep.

But Gilbert wakes while the night is dark –
    A restless sleeper aye,
He has heard the sound of a sheep-dog's bark,
    And his horse's warning neigh,
And he says to his mate, 'There are hawks abroad,
    And it's time we went away.'

Their rifles stood at the stretcher head,
    Their bridles lay to hand;
They wakened the old man out of his bed,
    When they heard the sharp command:
'In the name of the Queen lay down your arms,
    Now, Dunn and Gilbert, stand!'

Then Gilbert reached for his rifle true
    That close at hand he kept;
He pointed straight at the voice, and drew,
    But never a flash outleapt,
For the water ran from the rifle breech –
    It was drenched while the outlaws slept.

Then he dropped the piece with a bitter oath,
    And he turned to his comrade Dunn:
'We are sold,' he said, 'we are dead men both,
    But there may be a chance for one;
I'll stop and I'll fight with the pistol here,
    You take to your heels and run.'

So Dunn crept out on his hands and knees
 In the dim, half-dawning light,
And he made his way to a patch of trees,
 And was lost in the black of night;
And the trackers hunted his tracks all day,
 But they never could trace his flight.

But Gilbert walked from the open door
 In a confident style, and rash;
He heard at his side the rifles roar,
 And he heard the bullets crash.
But he laughed as he lifted his pistol-hand,
 And he fired at the rifle flash.

Then out of the shadows the troopers aimed
 At his voice and the pistol sound.
With rifle flashes the darkness flamed –
 He staggered and spun around,
And they riddled his body with rifle balls
 As it lay on the blood-soaked ground.

There's never a stone at the sleeper's head,
 There's never a fence beside,
And the wandering stock on the grave may tread
 Unnoticed and undenied;
But the smallest child on the Watershed
 Can tell you how Gilbert died.

A Bushman's Song

I'm travellin' down the Castlereagh, and I'm a station-hand;
I'm handy with the ropin'-pole, I'm handy with the brand,
And I can ride a rowdy colt, or swing the axe all day,
But there's no demand for a station-hand along the Castlereagh.

So it's shift, boys, shift, for there isn't the slightest doubt
That we've got to make a shift to the stations further out,

With the packhorse runnin' after, for he follows like a dog,
We must strike across the country at the old jig-jog.

This old black horse I'm riding – if you'll notice what's his
   brand,
He wears the crooked R, you see – none better in the land.
He takes a lot of beatin' and the other day we tried,
For a bit of a joke, with a racing bloke, for twenty pounds
   a side.

It was shift, boys, shift, for there wasn't the slightest doubt
That I had to make him shift, for the money was nearly out;
But he cantered home a winner, with the other one at the flog –
He's a red-hot sort to pick up with his old jig-jog.

I asked a cove for shearin' once along the Marthaguy:
'We shear non-union here,' says he. 'I call it scab,' says I.
I looked along the shearin' floor before I turned to go –
There were eight or ten dashed Chinamen a-shearin' in a row.

It was shift, boys, shift, for there wasn't the slightest doubt
It was time to make a shift with the leprosy about.
So I saddled up my horses, and I whistled to my dog,
And I left his scabby station at the old jig-jog.

I went to Illawarra, where my brother's got a farm;
He has to ask his landlord's leave before he lifts his arm;
The landlord owns the countryside – man, woman, dog, and cat,
They haven't the cheek to dare to speak without they touch
   their hat.

It was shift, boys, shift, for there wasn't the slightest doubt
Their little landlord god and I would soon have fallen out;
Was I to touch my hat to him? – was I his bloomin' dog?
So I makes for up the country at the old jig-jog.

But it's time that I was movin', I've a mighty way to go
Till I drink artesian water from a thousand feet below;

Till I meet the overlanders with the cattle comin' down –
And I'll work a while till I make a pile, then have a spree in
  town.

So, it's shift, boys, shift, for there isn't the slightest doubt
We've got to make a shift to the stations further out:
The packhorse runs behind us, for he follows like a dog,
And we cross a lot of country at the old jig-jog.

How Dacey Rode the Mule

'Twas to a small, up-country town,
  When we were boys at school,
There came a circus with a clown,
  Likewise a bucking mule.
The clown announced a scheme they had
  Spectators for to bring –
They'd give a crown to any lad
  Who'd ride him round the ring.

And, gentle reader, do not scoff
  Nor think a man a fool –
To buck a porous-plaster off
  Was pastime to that mule.

The boys got on; he bucked like sin;
  He threw them in the dirt.
What time the clown would raise a grin
  By asking, 'Are you hurt?'
But Johnny Dacey came one night,
  The crack of all the school;
Said he, 'I'll win the crown all right;
  Bring in your bucking mule.'

The elephant went off his trunk,
  The monkey played the fool,
And all the band got blazing drunk
  When Dacey rode the mule.

But soon there rose a galling shout
    Of laughter, for the clown
From somewhere in his pants drew out
    A little paper crown.
He placed the crown on Dacey's head
    While Dacey looked a fool;
'Now there's your crown, my lad,' he said,
    'For riding of the mule!'

The band struck up with 'Killaloe,'
    And 'Rule Britannia, Rule,'
And 'Young Man from the Country,' too,
    When Dacey rode the mule.

Then Dacey, in a furious rage,
    For vengeance on the show
Ascended to the monkeys' cage
    And let the monkeys go;
The blue-tailed ape and chimpanzee
    He turned abroad to roam;
Good faith! It was a sight to see
    The people step for home.

For big baboons with canine snout
    Are spiteful, as a rule –
The people didn't sit it out,
    When Dacey rode the mule.

And from the beasts he let escape,
    The bushmen all declare,
Were born some creatures partly ape
    And partly native-bear.
They're rather few and far between,
    The race is nearly spent;
But some of them may still be seen
    In Sydney Parliament.

And when those legislators fight,
And drink, and act the fool,
Just blame it on that torrid night
When Dacey rode the mule.

A Bush Christening

On the outer Barcoo where the churches are few,
And men of religion are scanty,
On a road never cross'd 'cept by folk that are lost
One Michael Magee had a shanty.

Now this Mike was the dad of a ten-year-old lad,
Plump, healthy, and stoutly conditioned;
He was strong as the best, but poor Mike had no rest
For the youngster had never been christened.

And his wife used to cry, 'If the darlin' should die
Saint Peter would not recognize him.'
But by luck he survived till a preacher arrived,
Who agreed straightaway to baptize him.

Now the artful young rogue, while they held their collogue,
With his ear to the keyhole was listenin';
And he muttered in fright, while his features turned white,
'What the divil and all is this christenin'?'

He was none of your dolts – he had seen them brand colts,
And it seemed to his small understanding,
If the man in the frock made him one of the flock,
It must mean something very like branding.

So away with a rush he set off for the bush,
While the tears in his eyelids they glistened –
''Tis outrageous,' says he, 'to brand youngsters like me;
I'll be dashed if I'll stop to be christened!'

Like a young native dog he ran into a log,
    And his father with language uncivil,
Never heeding the 'praste', cried aloud in his haste
    'Come out and be christened, you divil!'

But he lay there as snug as a bug in a rug,
    And his parents in vain might reprove him,
Till His Reverence spoke (he was fond of a joke),
    'I've a notion,' says he, 'that'll move him.'

'Poke a stick up the log, give the spalpeen a prog;
    Poke him aisy – don't hurt him or maim him;
'Tis not long that he'll stand, I've the water at hand,
    As he rushes out this end I'll name him.

'Here he comes, and for shame ye've forgotten the name –
    Is it Patsy or Michael or Dinnis?'
Here the youngster ran out, and the priest gave a shout –
    'Take your chance, anyhow, wid "Maginnis"!'

As the howling young cub ran away to the scrub
    Where he knew that pursuit would be risky,
The priest, as he fled, flung a flask at his head
    That was labelled 'Maginnis's Whisky!'

Now Maginnis Magee has been made a J.P.,
    And the one thing he hates more than sin is
To be asked by the folk, who have heard of the joke,
    How he came to be christened Maginnis!

The Man from Ironbark

It was the man from Ironbark who struck the Sydney town,
He wandered over street and park, he wandered up and down.
He loitered here, he loitered there, till he was like to drop,
Until at last in sheer despair he sought a barber's shop.
''Ere! shave my beard and whiskers off, I'll be a man of mark,
I'll go and do the Sydney toff up home in Ironbark.'

The barber man was small and flash, as barbers mostly are,
He wore a strike-your-fancy sash, he smoked a huge cigar:
He was a humorist of note and keen at repartee,
He laid the odds and kept a 'tote,' whatever that may be.
And when he saw our friend arrive, he whispered 'Here's a lark!
Just watch me catch him all alive this man from Ironbark.'

There were some gilded youths that sat along the barber's wall,
Their eyes were dull, their heads were flat, they had no brains
    at all;
To them the barber passed the wink, his dexter eyelid shut,
'I'll make this bloomin' yokel think his bloomin' throat is cut.'
And as he soaped and rubbed it in he made a rude remark:
'I s'pose the flats is pretty green up there in Ironbark.'

A grunt was all reply he got; he shaved the bushman's chin,
Then made the water boiling hot and dipped the razor in.
He raised his hand, his brow grew black, he paused a while to
    gloat,
Then slashed the red-hot razor-back across his victim's throat;
Upon the newly-shaven chin it made a livid mark –
No doubt it fairly took him in – the man from Ironbark.

He fetched a wild up-country yell might wake the dead to hear,
And though his throat, he knew full well, was cut from ear to ear,
He struggled gamely to his feet, and faced the murderous foe.
'You've done for me! you dog, I'm beat! one hit before I go!
I only wish I had a knife, you blessed murdering shark!
But you'll remember all your life the man from Ironbark.'

He lifted up his hairy paw, with one tremendous clout
He landed on the barber's jaw, and knocked the barber out.
He set to work with tooth and nail, he made the place a wreck;
He grabbed the nearest gilded youth, and tried to break his neck.
And all the while his throat he held to save his vital spark,
And 'Murder! Bloody Murder!' yelled the man from Ironbark.

A peeler man who heard the din came in to see the show;
He tried to run the bushman in, but he refused to go.
And when at last the barber spoke, and said ''Twas all in fun –
'Twas just a harmless little joke, a trifle overdone.'
'A joke!' he cried, 'By George, that's fine; a lively sort of lark;
I'd like to catch that murdering swine some night in Ironbark.'

And now while round the shearing-floor the listening shearers
    gape,
He tells the story o'er and o'er, and brags of his escape.
'Them barber chaps what keeps a tote, by George, I've had
    enough,
One tried to cut my bloomin' throat, but thank the Lord it's
    tough.'
And whether he's believed or no, there's one thing to remark,
That flowing beards are all the go way up in Ironbark.

It's Grand to be a Squatter

It's grand to be a squatter
    And sit upon a post,
And watch your little ewes and lambs
    A-giving up the ghost.

It's grand to be a 'cockie'
    With wife and kids to keep,
And find an all-wise Providence
    Has mustered all your sheep.

It's grand to be a Western man,
    With shovel in your hand,
To dig your little homestead out
    From underneath the sand.

It's grand to be a shearer
    Along the Darling-side,
And pluck the wool from stinking sheep
    That some days since have died.

It's grand to be a rabbit
  And breed till all is blue,
And then to die in heaps because
  There's nothing left to chew.

It's grand to be a Minister
  And travel like a swell,
And tell the Central District folk
  To go to – Inverell.

It's grand to be a socialist
  And lead the bold array
That marches to prosperity
  At seven bob a day.

It's grand to be an unemployed
  And lie in the Domain,
And wake up every second day –
  And go to sleep again.

It's grand to borrow English tin
  To pay for wharves and docks,
And then to find it isn't in
  The little money-box.

It's grand to be a democrat
  And toady to the mob,
For fear that if you told the truth
  They'd hunt you from your job.

It's grand to be a lot of things
  In this fair Southern land,
But if the Lord would send us rain,
  That would, indeed, be grand!

Waltzing Matilda

Once a jolly swagman camped by a billabong,
  Under the shade of a coolibah tree,
And he sang as he watched and waited till his billy boiled,
  'Who'll come a-waltzing Matilda with me?
    Waltzing Matilda,
    Waltzing Matilda,
  Who'll come a-waltzing Matilda with me?'
And he sang as he watched and waited till his billy boiled,
  'Who'll come a-waltzing Matilda with me?'

Down came a jumbuck to drink at the billabong:
  Up jumped the swagman and grabbed him with glee.
And he sang as he shoved that jumbuck in his tucker-bag,
  'You'll come a-waltzing Matilda with me.
    Waltzing Matilda,
    Waltzing Matilda,
  You'll come a-waltzing Matilda with me.'
And he sang as he shoved that jumbuck in his tucker-bag,
  'You'll come a-waltzing Matilda with me.'

Up rode a squatter, mounted on his thoroughbred;
  Down came the troopers, one, two, three:
'Whose' that jolly jumbuck you've got in your tucker-bag?
  You'll come a-waltzing Matilda with me!
    Waltzing Matilda,
    Waltzing Matilda,
  You'll come a-waltzing Matilda with me.
Whose' that jolly jumbuck you've got in your tucker-bag?
  You'll come a-waltzing Matilda with me!'

Up jumped the swagman and sprang into the billabong;
  'You'll never catch me alive!' said he;
And his ghost may be heard as you pass by that billabong,
  'You'll come a-waltzing Matilda with me!
    Waltzing Matilda,
    Waltzing Matilda,

You'll come a-waltzing Matilda with me!'
And his ghost may be heard as you pass by that billabong,
    'You'll come a-waltzing Matilda with me!'

E. J. BRADY (1869-1952)

Born at Carcoar in New South Wales, Brady received his early
education in the United States but returned to Australia at the
age of thirteen. He wandered over much of the country as
farmer, journalist, and bush-worker before settling down at
Mallacoota Inlet, Victoria, where he died.

The Western Road

My camp was by the Western Road – so new and yet so old –
The track the bearded diggers trod in roaring days of old;
The road Macquarie and his wife, a hundred years ago,
With warlike guard and retinue, went down in regal show.

The moon had silvered all the Bush; now, like an arc-light high,
She flickered in a scattered scud that dimmed the lower sky;
And, dreaming by my dying fire, whose embers fainter glowed,
I saw their shadows flitting by – the People of the Road.

I heard the clank of iron chains, and, as an evil blast
From some tormented nether world, the convict gangs went past
With sneering lips and leering eyes – grey ghosts of buried crime,
Who built a way for honest feet to tread in later time.

I caught the cruel click of steel; the trained and measured tread
Of soldiers of King George the Third, in coats of British red;
The moon upon their muskets gleamed, as, marching two by two,
They might have marched in better case the eve of Waterloo.

But, dreaming by my campfire still, uprose the merry horn;
A heavy stage came lumbering up from Penrith in the morn,
In beaver hats, the gentlemen their driver sat beside,
And ladies in hooped petticoats and quaint chignons inside.

T-ran-ta-ra! Blue Mountains hills re-echoed as they sung
A lilt of love and long ago – when all the world was young.
T-ran-ta-ra! Their shades went by, the bravest and the best,
The first Australian pioneers – whose graves are in the west.

A night wind whispered in the gums; afar out went the cry
Of mourning curlews on the flats, as madly galloped by
A fugitive with pallid face and pistol butt to hand,
And, hard behind with ringing hoofs, a close pursuing band.

Then – well remembered in my dream – a picture came to me
Of bitter fruit that ripened once upon a roadside tree;
How travellers shunned the haunted spot and evermore forbode
To camp beside the hangman's tree along the Western Road . . .

White-tilted in the moonlight went rough wagons one by one,
Piled high with household goods and stores of settlers dead and
    gone –
Blithe British yeomen and their wives, and sons of younger sons,
Who took tradition to the west, and axes, ploughs and guns.

These new-chum settlers tramped beside their dusty, creaking
    teams,
Their minds were filled with marvels new and golden hopes and
    dreams;
Their sons' tall sons still yeomen be, but mostly in the west
They ride their silken thoroughbreds, and ruffle with the best.

A motley crowd of eager folk, with tools and tents in fold
Came on Adventure's early quest to Gulgong, grief and gold;
They passed me in a jostling host, with anger or with mirth,
The fortune-seekers gathered from the ends of all the earth.

Yea, sailormen and tailormen, and prostitutes and peers,
Some honest and of good intent, some rogues and buccaneers.
Their campfires lit the darkened range, where, by the creeks, they
    lay
And dreamed of nuggets in their sleep – impatient for the day.

Came down the road a swaying coach, with troopers 'hind and
    fore –
The mounted escort thundered on by Lapstone Hill once more,
Their rifles at the shoulder slung, their scabbards long and bright;
They swung around the mountainside and rumbled out of sight.

Came up the road a swaying coach; his ribbons holding free,
The perfect driver tilted back his cherished cabbage-tree.
His girl will meet him at the rails tonight in Hartley Vale –
So, clear the track, and let her pass, the mid-Victorian mail!

Long shadows fell across the road; the mopoke in the still
And solemn midnight voiced aloud his warnings on the hill.
Yet, tramping slow and riding fast along that winding track,
The People of the Road went west, and coached and footed back.

My campfire died in ashes grey, as through my dream there went
That strange procession of the Past, on pay or plunder bent;
The teamsters, drovers, swagsmen, lags; the lovers and the
     thieves –
Until the east was red with dawn, the dew upon their leaves.

They vanished with the haunted night; their hope and high
     desire
As ashen as the grey, cold heap that erstwhile made my fire.
Across the tree-tops in the morn the golden sunlight showed;
And clearly rose another day – along the Western Road.

Lost and Given Over

The Hoogli gal 'er face is brown;
The Hilo gal is lazy;
The gal that lives by 'Obart town,
She'd drive a dead man crazy;
Come, wet your lip, and let it slip!
The *Gretna Green*'s a tidy ship –
Sing rally!
The seas is deep; the seas is blue;
But 'ere's good 'ealth to me and you!
Ho, rally!

The Lord may drop us off our pins
To feed 'is bloomin' fishes;
But Lord forgive us for our sins –
Our sins is most delicious!
Come, drink it up and fill yer cup!
The world it owes us bite and sup,
And Mimi, Ju-ju, Sally;
The seas is long; the winds is strong;
The best of men they *will* go wrong –
Hi, rally! ri-a-rally!

The Bowery gal she knows 'er know;
The Frisco gal is silly;
The Hayti girl ain't white as snow –
They're whiter down in Chili.
Now what's the use to shun the booze?
They'll flop yer bones among the ooze
Sou'-west-by-sou' the galley.
The seas is green; the seas is cold;
The best of men they must grow old –
Sing rally! ri-a-rally!

All round the world, where'er I roam,
This lesson I am learnin'.
If you've got sense you'll stop at home
And save the bit yer earnin'.
So hang the odds! Its little odds,
When every 'eathen 'as 'is gods,
An' neither two will tally:
When black and white drink, wimmin fight –
In these three things they're all alright –
Sing rally! ri-a-rally!

When double bunks, fo'castle end,
Is all the kind that's carried,
Our manners they will likely mend –
Most likely we'll be married.
But till sich time as that be done,
We'll take our fun as we've begun –
Sing rally!

The flesh is weak; the world is wide;
The dead man 'e goes overside –
Sing rally! rally!

We're given and lost to the girls that wait
From Trinity to Whitsund'y,
From Sunda Strait to the Golden Gate
An' back to the Bay o' Fundy;
Oh, it's Mabel, Loo, and it's Nancy-Poo,
An' 'ere's good luck, an' I love you –
Sing rally!
Oh, it's cents an' dollars an' somebody hollers
The sun comes up an' the mornin' follers –
Sing rally!

We're given an' lost to the octoroon,
The Portuguese cruiser painty,
The Chinkie gal with 'er eyes 'arf-moon,
An' the Japanese darlin' dainty.
Oh, it's Tokio-town when the sun goes down,
It's 'arf-a-pint and it's 'arf-a-crown –
Sing rally!
'Er spars may lift an' 'er keel can shift,
When a man is done 'e's got to drift –
Sing rally! Ho rally!

The Hoogli gal 'er face is brown,
The Hilo gal's a daisy,
The gal that lives by 'Obart town
She'd drive a dead man crazy.
So, pretty an' plain, it's Sarah Jane
'Uggin' an' kissin' an' 'Come again!'
Sing rally! ri-a-rally!
The seas is deep; the seas is wide;
But this I'll prove what else betide,
I'm bully *in* the alley,
Ho! Bull-*ee* in the Al-*lee*.

Homeward Bound

They will take us from the moorings, they will tow us down
   the Bay,
They will pluck us up to windward when we sail.
We shall hear the keen wind whistle, we shall feel the sting
   of spray,
When we've dropped the deep-sea pilot o'er the rail.
Then it's Johnnie heave an' start her, then it's Johnnie roll
   and go;
When the mates have picked the watches, there is little rest
   for Jack.
But we'll raise the good old chanty that the Homeward-
   bounders know,
For the girls have got the tow-rope, an' they're hauling in
   the slack.

In the dusty streets and dismal, through the noises of the
   town,
We can hear the West wind humming through the shrouds;
We can see the lightning leaping when the tropic suns go
   down,
And the dapple of the shadows of the clouds.
And the salt blood dances in us, to the tune of Homeward-
   Bound.
To the call to weary watches, to the sheet and to the tack.
When they bid us man the capstan how the hands will walk
   her round! –
For the girls have got the tow-rope, an' they're hauling in
   the slack.

Through the sunshine of the tropics, round the bleak and
   dreary Horn,
Half across the little planet lies our way.
We shall leave the land behind us like a welcome that's
   outworn
When we see the reeling mastheads swing and sway.

Through the weather fair or stormy, in the calm and in the
    gale,
We shall heave and haul to help her, we shall hold her on
    her track,
And you'll hear the chorus rolling when the hands are
    making sail,
For the girls have got the tow-rope, an' they're hauling in
    the slack!

KEIGHLEY GOODCHILD

Under the pen-name of 'Keighley', Goodchild published a
volume of verse in 1883 at Echuca, then Victoria's chief inland
port on the Murray in the period when the navigation of the
inland rivers was booming.

A Nautical Yarn

I sing of a captain who's well known to fame;
A naval commander, Bill Jinks is his name.
Who sailed where the Murray's clear waters do flow,
Did this freshwater shellback, with his Yeo heave a yeo.

To the port of Wahgunyah his vessel was bound,
When night came upon him and darkness around;
Not a star on the waters its clear light did throw;
But the vessel sped onward, with a Yeo heave a yeo.

'Oh! captain, Oh! captain, let's make for the shore,
For the winds they do rage and the waves do roar!'
'Nay, nay!' said the captain, 'though the fierce winds
    may blow,
I will stick to my vessel, with a Yeo heave a yeo.'

'Oh! captain, Oh! captain, the waves sweep the deck;
Oh! captain, Oh! captain, we'll soon be a wreck –
To the river's deep bosom each seaman will go!'
But the captain laughed loudly, with his Yeo heave a yeo.

'Farewell to the maiden – the girl I adore;
Farewell to my friends – I shall see them no more!'
The crew shrieked with terror, the captain he swore –
They had stuck on a sandbank, so they all walked ashore.

THOMAS E. SPENCER (1845-1910)

Born in London, Spencer came to Australia at the age of eighteen
but returned to England soon afterwards. He came back to live in
Australia in 1875.

How McDougal Topped the Score

A peaceful spot is Piper's Flat. The folk that live around –
They keep themselves by keeping sheep and turning up the
    ground;
But the climate is erratic, and the consequences are
The struggle with the elements is everlasting war.
We plough, and sow, and harrow – then sit down and pray for
    rain;
And then we all get flooded out and have to start again.
But the folk are now rejoicing as they ne'er rejoiced before,
For we've played Molongo cricket, and McDougal topped the
    score!

Molongo had a head on it, and challenged us to play
A single-innings match for lunch — the losing team to pay;
We were not great guns at cricket, but we couldn't well say no,
So we all began to practise, and we let the reaping go.
We scoured the Flat for ten miles round to muster up our men,
But when the list was totalled we could only number ten.
Then up spoke big Tim Brady: he was always slow to speak,
And he said – 'What price McDougal, who lives down at
    Cooper's Creek?'

So we sent for old McDougal, and he stated in reply
That he'd never played at cricket, but he'd half a mind to try.
He couldn't come to practise – he was getting in his hay,
But he guessed he'd show the beggars from Molongo how to play.
Now, McDougal was a Scotchman, and a canny one at that,
So he started in to practise with a paling for a bat.
He got Mrs Mac to bowl to him, but she couldn't run at all,
So he trained his sheep-dog, Pincher, how to scout and fetch
    the ball.

Now, Pincher was no puppy; he was old, and worn, and grey;
But he understood McDougal, and – accustomed to obey –
When McDougal cried out 'Fetch it!' he would fetch it in a trice,
But, until the word was 'Drop it!' he would grip it like a vice.
And each succeeding night they played until the light grew dim:
Sometimes McDougal struck the ball – sometimes the ball struck
    him.
Each time he struck, the ball would plough a furrow in the
    ground;
And when he missed, the impetus would turn him three times
    round.

The fatal day at last arrived – the day that was to see
Molongo bite the dust, or Piper's Flat knocked up a tree!
Molongo's captain won the toss, and sent his men to bat,
And they gave some leather-hunting to the men of Piper's Flat.
When the ball sped where McDougal stood, firm planted in his
    track,
He shut his eyes, and turned him round, and stopped it with
    his back!
The highest score was twenty-two, the total sixty-six,
When Brady sent a yorker down that scattered Johnson's sticks.

Then Piper's Flat went in to bat, for glory and renown,
But, like the grass before the scythe, our wickets tumbled down.
'Nine wickets down, for seventeen, with fifty more to win!'
Our captain heaved a sigh, and sent McDougal in.
'Ten pounds to one you'll lose it!' cried a barracker from town;
But McDougal said, 'I'll tak' it, mon!' and planted the money
    down.
Then he girded up his moleskins in a self-reliant style,
Threw off his hat and boots and faced the bowler with a smile.

He held the bat the wrong side out, and Johnson with a grin
Stepped lightly to the bowling crease, and sent a 'wobbler' in;
McDougal spooned it softly back, and Johnson waited there,
But McDougal, crying '*Fetch it!*' started running like a hare.
Molongo shouted 'Victory! He's out as sure as eggs,'

When Pincher started through the crowd, and ran through John-
    son's legs.
He seized the ball like lightning; then he ran behind a log,
And McDougal kept on running, while Molongo chased the dog!

They chased him up, they chased him down, they chased him
    round, and then
He darted through the slip-rail as the scorer shouted 'Ten!'
McDougal puffed; Molongo swore; excitement was intense;
As the scorer marked down twenty, Pincher cleared a barbed-
    wire fence.
'Let us head him!' shrieked Molongo. 'Brain the mongrel with
    a bat!'
'Run it out! Good old McDougal!' yelled the men of Piper's Flat.
And McDougal kept on jogging, and then Pincher doubled back,
And the scorer counted '*Forty*' as they raced across the track.

McDougal's legs were going fast, Molongo's breath was gone –
But still Molongo chased the dog – McDougal struggled on.
When the scorer shouted '*Fifty*', then they knew the chase could
    cease;
And McDougal gasped out 'Drop it!' as he dropped within his
    crease.
Then Pincher dropped the ball, and as instinctively he knew
Discretion was the wiser plan, he disappeared from view;
And as Molongo's beaten men exhausted lay around
We raised McDougal shoulder-high, and bore him from the
    ground.

We bore him to McGinniss's where lunch was ready laid,
And filled him up with whisky-punch, for which Molongo paid.
We drank his health in bumpers and we cheered him three times
    three,
And when Molongo got its breath Molongo joined the spree.
And the critics say they never saw a cricket match like that,
When McDougal broke the record in the game at Piper's Flat;
And the folk are jubilating as they never did before;
For we played Molongo cricket – and McDougal topped the
    score!

J. W. GORDON ('JIM GRAHAME') (1874-1949)

Born at Creswick on the Victorian gold-fields, J.W. Gordon spent much of his life in the outback and is said to have carried his swag with Henry Lawson.

Whalan of Waitin'-a-While

Long life to old Whalan of Waiting'-a-While;
    Good luck to his children and wife;
They gain all the pleasure and gladness that come
    And miss all the worries of life.
They do not complain if the season is dry.
    They go into debt with a smile.
'It's no use of moaning, it might have been worse,'
    Says Whalan of Waiting'-a-While.

The gates on the boundary fences are down
    And buried in rubbish and dust;
The white ants and weevils have eaten the rungs,
    The hinges are rotting with rust.
The sheep wander in, and the sheep wander out
    And ramble for many a mile:
'I must take a day off and fix up those gates,'
    Says Whalan of Waitin'-a-While.

The pigs roam at large, but they come home at night
    And sleep head and tail by the door,
And sometimes a sow has a litter of pigs
    That sleep with her under the floor.
They suckle and squabble around her all night,
    The odours arising are vile;
'We'll sell them right out when a buyer comes up,'
    Says Whalan of Waitin'-a-While.

The brand on the calves is as big as a plate
    And looks like a slash or a wale,
And sometimes it reaches from shoulder to hip,
    And sometimes it reaches the tail.

'Twas made from the side of a square iron tank,
 Cut out with a chisel or file,
'It's not very neat, but it might have been worse,'
 Says Whalan of Waitin'-a-While.

The boys and the girls all at riding excel,
 They stick to a saddle like glue,
And follow a bullock through low mulga scrub
 As straight as a die and as true.
They're no good at figures and can't read at all,
 Nor write in an elegant style.
'We'll give them a bit of a schooling some day,'
 Says Whalan of Waitin'-a-While.

The tanks and the dams very seldom get full,
 No matter how heavy it rains;
They've a halo of bones of the sheep that have bogged,
 And the dust-storms have silted the drains.
Storm-water is wasted and sweeps down the flat –
 A flood that would fill up the Nile –
'We'll clean out those drains when the weather gets cool,'
 Says Whalan of Waitin'-a-While.

The sulky and buggy stand out in the sun,
 The woodwork is gaping with cracks,
The leather is wrinkled and perishing fast,
 And pulling away from the tacks.
The wheels are all loose and the paint's falling off
 And the cushions have long lost their pile;
'I'd put up a shed, but I cannot find time,'
 Says Whalan of Waitin'-a-While.

Good luck to old Whalan of Waitin'-a-While.
 He'll live just as long as the rest,
And smile at the things that make most people frown,
 And his health is as good as the best.
Good luck to the mother at Waitin'-a-While,
 Who waddles along with a smile;
She'll have a fine time when the good seasons come,
 And she doesn't mind Waitin'-a-While.

P. J. HARTIGAN ('JOHN O'BRIEN') (1879-1952)

Born at Yass, New South Wales, the Rev. Patrick Joseph Harti-
gan wrote poems published in *Around the Boree Log and Other
Verses* under the pen-name of 'John O'Brien'. Father Hartigan
spent much of his life as parish priest in farming communities in
the mid-west of New South Wales.

Said Hanrahan

'We'll all be rooned,' said Hanrahan
    In accents most forlorn
Outside the church ere Mass began
    One frosty Sunday morn.

The congregation stood about,
    Coat-collars to the ears,
And talked of stock and crops and drought
    As it had done for years.

'It's lookin' crook,' said Daniel Croke;
    'Bedad, it's cruke, me lad,
For never since the banks went broke
    Has seasons been so bad.'

'It's dry, all right,' said young O'Neil,
    With which astute remark
He squatted down upon his heel
    And chewed a piece of bark.

And so around the chorus ran,
    'It's keepin' dry, no doubt.'
'We'll all be rooned,' said Hanrahan,
    'Before the year is out.

'The crops are done; ye'll have your work
    To save one bag of grain;
From here way out to Back-o'-Bourke
    They're singin' out for rain.

'They're singin' out for rain,' he said,
   'And all the tanks are dry.'
The congregation scratched its head
   And gazed around the sky.

'There won't be grass, in any case,
   Enough to feed an ass;
There's not a blade on Casey's place
   As I came down to Mass.'

'If rain don't come this month,' said Dan,
   And cleared his throat to speak –
'We'll all be rooned,' said Hanrahan,
   'If rain don't come this week.'

A heavy silence seemed to steal
   On all at this remark;
And each man squatted on his heel,
   And chewed a piece of bark.

'We want an inch of rain, we do,'
   O'Neil observed at last;
But Croke 'maintained' we wanted two
   To put the danger past.

'If we don't get three inches, man,
   Or four to break this drought,
We'll all be rooned,' said Hanrahan,
   'Before the year is out.'

In God's good time down came the rain;
   And all the afternoon
On iron roof and window-pane
   It drummed a homely tune.

And through the night it pattered still,
   And lightsome, gladsome elves
On dripping spout and window-sill
   Kept talking to themselves.

It pelted, pelted all day long,
    A-singing at its work,
Till every heart took up the song
    Way out to Back-o'-Bourke.

And every creek a banker ran,
    And dams filled overtop;
'We'll all be rooned,' said Hanrahan,
    'If this rain doesn't stop.'

And stop it did, in God's good time:
    And spring came in to fold
A mantle o'er the hills sublime
    Of green and pink and gold.

And days went by on dancing feet,
    With harvest-hopes immense,
And laughing eyes beheld the wheat
    Nid-nodding o'er the fence.

And, oh, the smiles on every face,
    As happy lad and lass
Through grass knee-deep on Casey's place
    Went riding down to Mass.

While round the church in clothes genteel
    Discoursed the men of mark,
And each man squatted on his heel,
    And chewed his piece of bark.

'There'll be bush-fires for sure, me man,
    There will, without a doubt;
We'll all be rooned,' said Hanrahan,
    'Before the year is out.'

R. HOLT ('6″ x 8″')

The popular 'folk' character of much bush balladry of this period is indicated by the fact that practically nothing, beyond their names, is known of many balladists, even of prolific ones like 'Six by Eight' and 'Steele Grey'.

Lachlan Jack

AXEMEN? Gippslanders and Tassies?
    Sonny mine, you make me smile!
To those chopping guns you mention
    Lachlan Jack can give a mile!

What was that you whispered, sonny?
    Where the devil were you dried!
Never heard of Jack the Axeman,
    Over on the Lachlan-side?

Jack was bred on Weddin Mountains,
    And from Grenfell out to Bourke,
To him nought can hold the candle
    When it comes to timber-work!

Gidgee, myall, box and jarrah,
    Ironbark or mountain-gum!
He goes through 'em like a sawmill,
    And he downs 'em as they come!

Saw him chopping for a wager –
    He has not been beat as yet –
It was raining cats and dogs, and
    We were getting soaking wet.

But he swung his seven-pounder,
    And he caused the chips to fly
In such lightning succession
    That they kept him snug and dry!

G. M. SMITH ('STEELE GREY')

Post-Hole Mick

A short time back, while over in Vic.,
I met with a chap called Post-Hole Mick.
A raw-boned, loose-built son of a Paddy;
And at putting down post-holes he was a daddy!

And wherever you'd meet him, near or far,
He had always his long-handled shovel and bar.
(I suppose you all know what I mean by a bar?
It's a lump of wrought iron the shape of a spar.

With one chisel end for digging the ground,
Its average weight about twenty pound).
He worked for the cockies around Geelong,
And for some time they kept him going strong.

He would sink them a hundred holes for a bob,
And, of course, soon worked himself out of a job;
But when post-hole sinking got scarce for Mick,
He greased his brogues and cut his stick.

And one fine day he left Geelong,
And took his shovel and bar along;
He took to the track in search of work,
And struck due north, en route to Bourke.

It seems he had been some time on tramp,
When one day he struck a fencers' camp.
The contractor there was wanting a hand,
As post-hole sinkers were in demand.

He showed him the line, and put him on,
But while he looked round, sure Mick was gone –
There were the holes, but where was the man?
Then his eye along the line he ran.

Mick had already done ninety-nine,
And at hunting rate was running the line.
The Boss had some sinkers he thought were quick,
Till the day he engaged one, Post-Hole Mick.

When the job was finished, Mick started forth,
And appears to have set his course due north,
For I saw a report in the 'Croydon Star',
Where a fellow had passed with a shovel and bar.

To give an idea of how he could walk,
A day or two later he struck Cape York!
If they can't find him work there, putting down holes,
I'm afraid he'll arrive at one of the Poles!

W. T. GOODGE (1862-1909)

Goodge was a journalist who published a good deal of humorous verse collected in *Hits! Skits! and Jingles!*, published in 1899.

Versions of *The Great Australian Adjective* are known and recited by a great many people who have never heard of its author. This 'folk' version, which is a considerable improvement on the original, was current among undergraduates at the University of Adelaide in the 1930s.

The Great Australian Adjective

A sunburnt bloody stockman stood,
And in a dismal bloody mood,
  Apostrophized his bloody cuddy:
'This bloody moke's no bloody good,
He doesn't earn his bloody food.
  Bloody! Bloody! Bloody!'

He jumped across his bloody horse
And galloped off of bloody course,
  The road was wet and bloody muddy.
He road up hill, down bloody dale,
The wind, it blew a bloody gale.
  Bloody! Bloody! Bloody!

He came up to a bloody creek;
The bloody horse was bloody weak;
  The creek was full and bloody floody.
He said, 'This moke must sink or swim,
The same for me as bloody him:
  Bloody! Bloody! Bloody!'

He plunged into the bloody creek:
The horse it gave a bloody shriek:
  The stockman's face a bloody study,
Ejaculating as they sank,
Before they reached the bloody bank:
  'Bloody! Bloody! Bloody!'

WILL H. OGILVIE (1869-1963)

Born in Scotland, Ogilvie spent only twelve years in Australia –
from 1889 to 1901. This happened to be the period when the
bush ballad was a new and exciting phenomenon. The young
Scotsman spent these impressionable years in western Queens-
land, New South Wales, and Victoria, trying his hand at horse-
breaking, droving, and other bush work. He thus became
thoroughly Australian in sentiment and continued, after his
return to Scotland, to write and publish prolifically on outback
themes.

We've Been Droving Too

Store cattle from Nelanjie! The mob goes feeding past,
With half-a-mile of sandhill 'twixt the leaders and the last;
The nags that move behind them are the good old Queensland
    stamp –
Short backs and perfect shoulders that are priceless on a camp;
And these are *Men* that ride them, broad-chested, tanned, and
    tall,
The bravest hearts amongst us and the lightest hands of all:
Oh, let them wade in Wonga grass and taste the Wonga dew,
And let them spread, those thousand head – for we've been
    droving too!

Store cattle from Nelanjie! By half-a-hundred towns,
By northern ranges rough and red, by rolling open downs,
By stock-routes brown and burnt and bare, by flood-wrapped
    river-bends,
They've hunted them from gate to gate – the drover has no
    friends!
But idly they may ride today beneath the scorching sun
And let the hungry bullocks try the grass on Wonga run;
No overseer will dog them here to 'see the cattle through',
But they may spread their thousand head – for we've been droving
    too!

Store cattle from Nelanjie! They've a naked track to steer;
The stockyards at Wodonga are a long way down from here;

The creeks won't run till God knows when, and half the holes
    are dry;
The tanks are few and far between and water's dear to buy:
There's plenty at the Brolga bore for all his stock and mine –
We'll pass him with a brave God-speed across the Border Line;
And if he goes a five-mile stage and loiters slowly through,
We'll only think the more of him – for we've been droving too!

Store cattle from Nelanjie! They're mute as milkers now;
But yonder grizzled drover, with the care-lines on his brow,
Could tell of merry musters on the big Nelanjie plains,
With blood upon the chestnut's flanks and foam upon the reins;
Could tell of nights upon the road when those same mild-eyed
    steers
Went ringing round the river-bend and through the scrub like
    spears;
And if his words are rude and rough, we know his words are true,
We know what wild Nelanjies are – and we've been droving too!

Store cattle from Nelanjie! Around the fire at night
They've watched the pine-tree shadows lift before the dancing
    light;
They've lain awake to listen when the weird bush-voices speak,
And heard the lilting bells go by along the empty creek;
They've spun the yarns of hut and camp, the tales of play and
    work,
The wondrous tales that gild the road from Normanton to
    Bourke;
They've told of fortunes foul and fair, of women false and true,
And well we know the songs they've sung – for we've been
    droving too!

Store cattle from Nelanjie! Their breath is on the breeze;
You hear them tread, a thousand head, in blue-grass to the knees;
The lead is on the netting-fence, the wings are spreading wide,
The lame and laggard scarcely move – so slow the drovers ride!
But let them stay and feed today for sake of Auld Lang Syne;
They'll never get a chance like this below the Border Line;
And if they tread our frontage down, what's that to me or you?
What's ours to fare, by God they'll share! for we've been droving too!

CHARLES SHAW (1900-55)

Born in Melbourne, Shaw became an orphan at the age of thirteen or fourteen. For the next fifteen years or so he roamed the Bush, shearing, timber-getting, fencing, boundary-riding, and so on. From 1938 until his death he worked as a journalist on the Sydney *Bulletin* and published a collection of verse, another of short stories, some children's books, a novel, *Heaven Knows, Mr Allison*, and four thrillers under the pen-name of 'Bant Singer'.

Though most of his verses look back to a legendary past time, Shaw has been placed in this section because of the direct, artless style which he shares with the balladists of the nineties. The anonymous bushman who rode the 'big white bull through Wagga' appears in many folk-tales.

The Search

I've dropped me swag in many camps
    From Queensland west to Boulder
An' struck all sorts of outback champs
    An' many a title-holder.
But though I've heard the episode
    By drover told, an' dogger,
I've still to meet the bloke who rode
    The big white bull through Wagga.

I struck the hero out at Hay
    Who beat the red-back spider
In fourteen rounds one burnin' day,
    An' up along the Gwydir
There lives the man outslept the toad –
    A champeen blanket-flogger –
But he is not the bloke who rode
    The big white bull through Wagga.

The cove that hung up Bogan Gate
    Once called me in a hurry
To buy drinks for his 'China plate',
    The bloke that dug the Murray.

An' though down south of Beechworth road
  I met big Bob the Frogger,
I've still to meet the bloke who rode
  The big white bull through Wagga.

The man who steered the kangaroo
  From Cue to Daly Waters;
The cove who raced the emu, too,
  To win three squatters' daughters;
I know the fellow moved the load
  That stopped the Richmond logger;
But still I want the bloke who rode
  The big white bull through Wagga.

But some fine day I'll run him down,
  An' stop his flamin' skitin'.
I'll punch him on his lyin' crown,
  Or go down gamely fightin'.
For *I'm* the bloke to whom is owed
  What's paid that limelight-hogger;
I'd *love* to meet that bloke who rode
  The big white bull through Wagga.

G. H. GIBSON ('IRONBARK') (1846-1921)

English-born, Gibson went to New Zealand at the age of twenty-three and on to New South Wales soon afterwards. As an inspector of the Department of Lands he travelled widely in the outback and came to know bush life intimately. His earlier published work helped, in some respects, to pave the way for the bush ballad of the nineties.

My Mate Bill

Jimmy the Hut-keeper speaks:
That's his saddle across the tie-beam, an' them's his spurs up there
On the wall-plate over yonder: you kin see's they ain't a pair.
The daddy of all stockmen as ever come musterin' here –
Killed in the flamin' mallee, yardin' a scrub-bred steer!

They say as he's gone to heaven, an' shook off his worldly cares,
But I can't sight Bill in a halo set up on three blinded hairs.
In heaven! What next, I wonder, for, strike me pink an' blue
If I savvy what in thunder they'll find for Bill to do!

He'd never make one o' them angels with faces white as chalk,
All wool to the toes, like hoggets, an' wings like a eagle'awk:
He couldn't 'arp for apples – his voice 'ad tones as jarred,
An' he'd no more ear than a bald-faced bull, or calves in a brandin'-yard.

He could sit on a buckin' brumby like a nob in an easy chair
An' chop his name with a green-hide fall on the flank of a flyin' steer;
He could show the saints in glory the way that a fall should drop,
But, sit on a throne! – not William – unless they could make it prop.

If the heavenly hosts get boxed now, as mobs most always will,
Why, who'd cut 'em out like William, or draft on the camp like Bill?

An 'orseman 'd find it awkward, at first, with a push that flew;
But blame my cats if I knows what else they'll find for Bill to do!

He mightn't freeze to the seraphs, or chum with the cherubim,
But if ever the seraph-johnnies get pokin' it, like, at him –
Well, if there's hide in heaven, an' silk for to make a lash,
He'll yard the lot in the Jasper Lake in a blinded lightnin'-flash!

It's hard if there ain't no cattle, but perhaps they'll let him sleep,
An' wake him up at the Judgment for to draft them goats an'
    sheep:
It's playin' it low on William, but perhaps he'll buckle-to,
Just to show them high-toned seraphs what a mallee-man can do.

If they saddles a big-boned angel, with a turn o' speed, of course,
As can spiel like a four-year brumby an' prop like an old camp-
    horse –
If they puts Bill up with a snaffle, an' a four or five-inch spur,
An' eighteen foot o' green-hide for to chop the blinded fur,
He'll draft them blamed Angoras in a way, it's safe to swear,
As'll make them toney seraphs sit back on their thrones an' stare!

E. G. MURPHY ('DRYBLOWER') (1867-1939)

Born (like the legendary 'Wild Colonial Boy') at Castlemaine,
Victoria, Murphy joined the thousands who left that colony
during the depression of the early 1890s for the gold-rush to
Western Australia. He dug for gold in the semi-desert for some
years and began to write ballads about the Western Australian
miners' life. Later he took up journalism in Perth.

A 'dryblower' is a crude device, made of hessian and wooden
saplings, and used in arid areas for separating gold from the ore.
As the miner shakes the framework of the 'dryblower', the wind
blows away the lighter earth leaving behind the heavy grains of
gold.

The Smiths

We had many problems set us when Coolgardie was a camp,
When the journey to the goldfields meant a coach-fare or a tramp;
We had water questions, tucker ditto, also that of gold,
How to clothe ourselves in summer, how to dress to dodge the
    cold.
We marvelled how the reefs occurred in most unlikely spots,
For the topsy-turvy strata tied geologists in knots;
But though we plumbed the depths of many mysteries and myths,
The worst we had to fathom was the prevalence of Smiths.

To say they swarmed Coolgardie was to say the very least,
For they over-ran the district like the rabbits in the East;
The name predominated in the underlay and drive,
The open-cut and costeen seemed to be with Smiths alive;
Where the dishes tossed the gravel they gathered from afar,
They clustered at the two-up school and at the shanty bar;
And while Jones and Brown were just as thick as herrings in a
    frith,
If you threw a stone at random, you were sure to hit a Smith.

There were Smiths from every region where the Smiths are
    known to grow,
There were cornstalk Smiths, Victorian Smiths, and Smiths who
    eat the crow;
There were Maori Smiths, Tasmanian Smiths, and parched-up
    Smiths from Cairns;
Bachelor Smiths and widower Smiths and Smiths with wives
    and bairns.
Some assumed the names for reasons that to them were known
    the best
When silently they packed their ports and flitted to the West,
Till every second man you met to yarn or argue with
Was either a legitimate or else a bogus Smith.

It really mattered little till the days the big mails came,
And then began the trouble with that far too-frequent name;
For the Smiths rolled up in regiments when the letter 'S' was
    called,
To drive the post-officials mad and prematurely bald.
Shoals of Smiths demanded letters that were never to them sent,
Wrong Smiths got correspondence which for them was never
    meant;
And many a Smith, whose facial calm shamed Egypt's monolith,
Bought jim-jams with the boodle sent to quite a different Smith.

The climax came one Christmas Eve, the mail was on its way,
And the post-officials yearned to block the Smiths on Christmas
    Day;
So they faked an Eastern telegram by methods justified,
Upon it put no Christian name and tacked it up outside;
It was from a Melbourne lawyer, and addressed to 'Smith,
    Esquire'
It was stamped 'prepaid and urgent', so 'twould confidence
    inspire,
And when Coolgardie sighted it and marked its pungent pith,
There was pallid consternation in the habitat of Smith.

'Our client has informed us you are over in the West,'
Ran the message, 'and she threatens your immediate arrest;
She hears you're known as Smith, but says you needn't be
    afraid
If you'll come and face the music and redeem the promise made.'
The population read it, and before the daylight came
A swarm of Smiths rolled up their swags and took a different
    name,
They declined to 'face the music' and return to kin and kith,
And the maidens who were promised still await the absent Smith.

Holus Bolus

He lay in the hospital, pallid and weak,
    The wreck of a once healthy man;
His breathing was wheezy, his voice was a squeak,
    As his story of woe he began.

''Twas Danny O'Hara,' he murmered in pain,
    'Who told me his camel was bad –
A bulky young bull, with the strength of a crane,
    But a temperament quiet and sad.

'O'Hara, who'd drifted from Kimberley down,
    Had scratched every field to Lefroy,
And shifted the country – red, yellow and brown –
    For the metal elusive and coy.

'Through seasons of flushness and seasons of "slate",
    He'd managed to battle and roam,
Unmoved by all offers to purchase the mate
    Whose hump he regarded as home.

'And the camel was sick – laid limp in his tracks,
    As his mother had laid, full of spears –
When Danny had shattered the phalanx of blacks,
    And wiped off a pile of arrears.

'O'Hara had left him at Cassidy's Hill,
  And he'd call me an angel from Heaven
If I'd help him to give him a pick-me-up pill
  And keep him from throwing a seven.

'A pipe was procured – three feet of bamboo –
  Then Danny, myself and the pill
Went bravely this medical office to do
  For the patient at Cassidy's Hill.

'"When the pill's in the pipe, and the pipe's in his jaws –
  Which I'll open," O'Hara observed –
"You'll place the free end of the blow-pipe in yours
  And puff when his gullet's uncurved.

'"I'd blow it myself, but my bellows are weak,
  For I've got a young winze in my lung;
Since I argued the point with the blacks at the Peak
  My puffing machinery's bung.

'"The pill is composed," he further explained,
  "Of axle-grease, sulphur and tar;
While a piquant and suitable flavour is gained
  By a dip in the kerosene jar.

'"To aid his digestion there's tin-tacks and shot,
  Then I've seasoned it strongly with snuff;
And I want in his system to scatter the lot,
  So take a deep breath when you puff."

'With the pipe to my lips a long 'un I drew,
  Till my diaphragm threatened to burst,
When, bang down my gullet the flaming pill flew,
  For the blithering camel blew first!'

HARRY MORANT ('THE BREAKER') (1865-1902)

Reputedly the black sheep of a well-connected Devon family, Morant drifted into the Australian outback in the eighties where he established a reputation, which still survives, for recklessness and daring. Like Adam Lindsay Gordon he is remembered in Australia almost as much for his legendary feats of horse-riding as for his poetry. He served in the Boer War as a lieutenant in the Bushveldt Carbineers, a highly irregular troop of cavalrymen. He was court-martialled and shot for having killed some Boer prisoners. He and his many admirers claimed that he was made a scapegoat for more highly-placed officers who had given orders that the unit was 'to take no prisoners'.

Stirrup Song

We've drunk our wine, we've kissed our girls, and funds are
    getting low,
The horses must be thinking its a fair thing now to go.
Sling up the swags on Condamine, and strap the billies fast,
And stuff a bottle in the bag, and let's be off at last.

What matter if the creeks are up! – the cash, alas, runs down! –
A very sure and certain sign we're long enough in town;
The nigger rides the 'boko', and you'd better take the bay,
Quartpot will do to carry me the stage we'll go today.

No grass this side the Border fence, and all the mulga's dead;
The horses for a day or two will have to spiel ahead;
Man never yet from Queensland brought a bullock or a hack
But lost condition on that God-abandoned Border track.

But once we're through the rabbit-proof, it's certain since the
    rain
There's whips of grass and water, so it's 'West-by-North' again;
There's feed on Tyson's country, we can spell the mokes a week
Where Billy Stevens last year trapped his brumbies, on Bough
    Creek.

The Paroo may be quickly crossed – the Eulo Common's bare –
And anyhow it isn't wise, old man, to dally there!
Alack-a-day! far wiser men than you or I succumb
To woman's wiles and potency of Queensland wayside rum!

Then over sand and spinifex! and on o'er range and plain!
The nags are fresh; besides they know they're westward-bound
    again!
The brand upon old Darkie's thigh is that upon the hide
Of bullocks we shall muster on the Diamantina side.

We'll light our campfires while we may, and yarn beside the
    blaze,
The jingling hobble-chains shall make a music through the days;
And while the tucker-bags are right and we've a stock of weed
The swagman will be welcome to a pipeful and a feed.

So fill your pipe, and ere we mount we'll drain a parting nip:
Here's now that West-by-North again may prove a lucky trip;
Then back once more, let's trust you'll find your best girl's
    merry face,
Or, if she jilts you, may you get a better in her place!

'The Breaker's' Last Rhyme and Testament

In prison cell I sadly sit –
A d – d crestfallen chappy!
And own to you I feel a bit –
A little bit – unhappy!

It really ain't the place nor time
To reel off rhyming diction –
But yet we'll write a final rhyme
While waiting cru-ci-fixion!

No matter what 'end' they decide –
'Quicklime? or b'iling ile? sir!'
We'll do our best when crucified
To finish off in style, sir!

But we bequeath a parting tip
For sound advice as such men
Who come across in transport ship
To polish off the Dutchmen!

If you encounter any Boers
You really must not loot 'em,
And if you wish to leave these shores
For pity's sake *don't shoot 'em!*

And if you'd earn a D.S.O. –
Why every British sinner
Should know the proper way to go
Is: '*Ask the Boer to dinner!*'

Let's toss a bumper down our throat
Before we pass to Heaven,
And toast: 'the trim-set petticoat
We leave behind in Devon.'

VICTOR J. DALEY (1858-1905)

Reaching Australia at the age of twenty, Daley did clerical and journalistic work in Adelaide, Melbourne, Sydney, Queanbeyan, and Grafton in which last-named country town he lived for a time with E. J. Brady. He died of tuberculosis.

As the poems below show, Daley shared fully in the democratic and utopian aspirations of the pre-federation decade, but most of his verse moves in a dream-like, lyrical world reminiscent of the 'Celtic twilight'. His *Ballad of Eureka* is one of many which show how the gold-fields 'rebellion' of 1854 was later taken up as a key symbol of the nationalist ferment of the nineties which issued in Australian Federation.

A Ballad of Eureka

Stand up, my young Australian,
　　In the brave light of the sun,
And hear how Freedom's battle
　　Was in old days lost – and won.
The blood burns in my veins, boy,
　　As it did in years of yore,
Remembering Eureka,
　　And the men of 'Fifty-four.

The Tyrants of the Goldfields
　　Would not let us live in peace;
They harried us and chased us
　　With their horse and foot police.
Each man must show his licence
　　When they chose, by fits and starts:
They tried to break our spirits,
　　And they almost broke our hearts.

There comes a time to all men
　　When submission is a sin;
We made a bonfire brave, and
　　Flung our licences therein.

Our hearts with scorn and anger
  Burned more fiercely than the flame,
Full well we knew our peril,
  But we dared it all the same.

On Bakery Hill the Banner
  Of the Southern Cross flew free;
Then up rose Peter Lalor,
  And with lifted hand spake he: –
'We swear by God above us,
  While we live, to work and fight
For Freedom and for Justice,
  For our Manhood and our Right.'

Then, on the bare earth kneeling,
  As on a chapel-floor,
Beneath the sacred Banner,
  One and all, that oath we swore:
And some of those who swore it
  Were like straws upon a flood,
But there were men who swore it
  And who sealed it with their blood.

I said, my young Australian,
  That the fight was lost – and won –
But, oh, our hearts were heavy
  At the setting of the sun.
Yet, ere the year was over,
  Freedom rolled in like a flood:
They gave us all we asked for –
  When we asked for it in blood.

The bitter fight was ended,
  And, with cruel coward-lust,
They dragged our sacred Banner
  Through the Stockade's bloody dust.

But, patient as the gods are,
　　Justice counts the years and waits -
That Banner now waves proudly
　　Over Six Australian States.

God rest you, Peter Lalor!
　　For you were a whiteman whole;
A swordblade in the sunlight
　　Was your bright and gallant soul.
And God reward you kindly,
　　Father Smith, alive or dead:
'Twas you that gave him shelter
　　When a price was on his head.

Within the Golden City
　　In the place of peace profound
The Heroes sleep. Tread softly:
　　'Tis Australia's Holy Ground.
And ever more Australia
　　Will keep green in her heart's core
The memory of Lalor
　　And the Men of 'Fifty-four.

The Parson and the Prelate

I saw a Parson on a bike -
A parody on things -
His coat-tails flapped behind him like
A pair of caudal wings.

His coat was of the shiny green,
His hat was rusty brown;
He was a weird, wild sight, I ween,
Careering through the town.

What perched him on a wheel at all,
And made him race and rip?

Had he, perchance, a sudden call
To some rich rectorship?

He'd no such call; he raced and ran
To kneel and pray beside
The bedside of a dying man,
Who poor as Peter died.

I saw a Prelate, plump and fine,
Who gleamed with sanctity;
He was the finest-groomed divine
That you would wish to see.

His smile was bland; his air was grand;
His coat was black, and shone
As did the tents of Kedar and
The robes of Solomon.

And in a carriage fine and fair
He lounged in lordly ease –
It was a carriage and a pair –
And nursed his gaitered knees.

And whither went he, and what for,
With all this pomp and show?
He went to see the Governor,
And that is all I know.

But in a vision of the night,
When deep dreams come to men,
I saw a strange and curious sight –
The Prelate once again.

He sat ungaitered, and undone,
A picture of dismay –
His carriage was too broad to run
Along the Narrow Way!

But, with his coat-tails flapping like
Black caudal wings in wrath,
I saw the Parson on the bike
Sprint up the Shining Path.

The Woman at the Washtub

The Woman at the Washtub,
   She works till fall of night;
With soap, and suds and soda
   Her hands are wrinkled white.
Her diamonds are the sparkles
   The copper-fire supplies;
Her opals are the bubbles
   That from the suds arise.

The Woman at the Washtub
   Has lost the charm of youth;
Her hair is rough and homely,
   Her figure is uncouth;
Her temper is like thunder,
   With no one she agrees –
The children of the alley
   They cling around her knees.

The Woman at the Washtub
   She too had her romance;
There was a time when lightly
   Her feet flew in the dance.
Her feet were silver swallows,
   Her lips were flowers of fire;
Then she was Bright and Early,
   The Blossom of Desire.

O Woman at the Washtub,
   And do you ever dream
Of all your days gone by in
   Your aureole of steam?

From birth till we are dying
   You wash our sordid duds,
O Woman of the Washtub!
   O Sister of the Suds!

One night I saw a vision
   That filled my soul with dread,
I saw a Woman washing
   The grave-clothes of the dead;
The dead were all the living,
   And dry were lakes and meres,
The Woman at the Washtub
   She washed them with her tears.

I saw a line with banners
   Hung forth in proud array –
The banners of all battles
   From Cain to Judgment Day.
And they were stiff with slaughter
   And blood, from hem to hem,
And they were red with glory,
   And she was washing them.

'Who comes forth to the Judgment,
   And who will doubt my plan?'
'I come forth to the Judgment
   And for the Race of Man.
I rocked him in his cradle,
   I washed him for his tomb,
I claim his soul and body,
   And I will share his doom.'

ANON

This ballad, which gives a reasonably accurate if highly partisan account of the death of Ben Hall the bushranger in 1865, has often been treated as just another anonymous old bush song. Fairly obviously, it is not this but rather a 'literary' ballad in the tradition of A.B. Paterson's *How Gilbert Died*. On internal stylistic grounds, it seems not unlikely to have been the work of Alice Werner, author of the next poem in this section.

The Death of Ben Hall

Ben Hall was out on the Lachlan side
With a thousand pounds on his head;
A score of troopers were scattered wide
And a hundred more were ready to ride
Wherever a rumour led.

They had followed his track from the Weddin heights
And north by the Weelong yards;
Through dazzling days and moonlit nights
They had sought him over their rifle-sights,
With their hands on their trigger-guards.

The outlaw stole like a hunted fox
Through the scrub and stunted heath,
And peered like a hawk from his eyrie rocks
Through the waving boughs of the sapling box
On the troopers riding beneath.

His clothes were rent by the clutching thorn
And his blistered feet were bare;
Ragged and torn, with his beard unshorn,
He hid in the woods like a beast forlorn,
With a padded path to his lair.

But every night when the white stars rose
He crossed by the Gunning Plain
To a stockman's hut where the Gunning flows,
And struck on the door three swift light blows,
And a hand unhooked the chain –

And the outlaw followed the lone path back
With food for another day;
And the kindly darkness covered his track
And the shadows swallowed him deep and black
Where the starlight melted away.

But his friend had read of the Big Reward,
And his soul was stirred with greed;
He fastened his door and window-board,
He saddled his horse and crossed the ford,
And spurred to the town at speed.

You may ride at a man's or a maid's behest
When honour or true love call
And steel your heart to the worst or best,
But the ride that is ta'en on a traitor's quest
Is the bitterest ride of all.

A hot wind blew from the Lachlan bank
And a curse on its shoulder came;
The pine trees frowned at him, rank on rank,
The sun on a gathering storm-cloud sank
And flushed his cheek with shame.

He reined at the Court; and the tale began
That the rifles alone should end;
Sergeant and trooper laid their plan
To draw the net on a hunted man
At the treacherous word of a friend.

False was the hand that raised the chain
And false was the whispered word:
'The troopers have turned to the south again,
You may dare to camp on the Gunning Plain.'
And the weary outlaw heard.

He walked from the hut but a quarter-mile
Where a clump of saplings stood
In a sea of grass like a lonely isle;
And the moon came up in a little while
Like silver steeped in blood.

Ben Hall lay down on the dew-wet ground
By the side of his tiny fire;
And a night-breeze woke, and he heard no sound
As the troopers drew their cordon round –
And the traitor earned his hire.

And nothing they saw in the dim grey light,
But the little glow in the trees;
And they crouched in the tall cold grass all night,
Each one ready to shoot at sight,
With his rifle cocked on his knees.

When the shadows broke and the dawn's white sword
Swung over the mountain wall,
And a little wind blew over the ford,
A sergeant sprang to his feet and roared:
'In the name of the Queen, Ben Hall!'

Haggard, the outlaw leapt from his bed
With his lean arms held on high.
'Fire!' And the word was scarcely said
When the mountains rang to a rain of lead –
And the dawn went drifting by.

They kept their word and they paid his pay
Where a clean man's hand would shrink;
And that was the traitor's master-day
As he stood by the bar on his homeward way
And called on the crowd to drink.

He banned no creed and he barred no class,
And he called to his friends by name;
But the worst would shake his head and pass
And none would drink from the bloodstained glass
And the goblet red with shame.

And I know when I hear the last grim call
And my mortal hour is spent,
When the light is hid and the curtains fall
I would rather sleep with the dead Ben Hall
Than go where that traitor went.

ALICE WERNER (1859-1935)

Born in Austria, Alice Werner spent part of her childhood in
New Zealand and, it would seem, in Australia. She worked for
some years at journalism and then taught, from 1917 till her
retirement in 1930, as lecturer and later professor of Swahili and
Bantu Languages in the University of London.

Bannerman of the Dandenong

I rode through the bush in the burning noon,
    Over the hills to my bride,
The track was rough and the way was long,
And Bannerman of the Dandenong,
    He rode along by my side.

A day's march off my Beautiful dwelt,
    By the Murray streams in the West;
Lightly lilting a gay love-song
Rode Bannerman of the Dandenong,
    With a blood-red rose on his breast.

'Red, red rose of the Western streams,'
    Was the song he sang that day –
Truest comrade in hour of need,
Bay Mathinna his peerless steed –
    I had my own good grey.

There fell a spark on the upland grass –
    The dry bush leapt into flame;
And I felt my heart go cold as death,
But Bannerman smiled and caught his breath,
    But I heard him name her name.

Down the hillside the fire-floods rushed,
    On the roaring eastern wind;
Neck and neck was the reckless race,
Ever the bay mare kept her pace,
    But the grey horse dropped behind.

He turned in the saddle – 'Let's change, I say!'
  And his bridle rein he drew.
He sprang to the ground, 'Look sharp!' he said
With a backward toss of his curly head –
  'I ride lighter than you!'

Down and up – it was quickly done –
  No words to waste that day!
Swift as a swallow she sped along,
The good bay mare from Dandenong,
  And Bannerman rode the grey.

The hot air scorched like a furnace blast
  From the very mouth of hell:
The blue gums caught and blazed on high
Like flaming pillars into the sky;
  The grey horse staggered and fell.

'Ride, ride, lad, ride for her sake!' he cried;
  Into the gulf of flame
Were swept, in less than a breathing space
The laughing eyes, and the comely face,
  And the lips that named *her* name.

She bore me bravely, the good bay mare;
  Stunned, and dizzy and blind;
I heard the sound of a mingling roar –
'Twas the Lachlan river that rushed before,
  And the flames that rolled behind.

Safe – safe, at Nammoora gate,
  I fell, and lay like a stone.
O love! thine arms were about me then,
Thy warm tears called me to life again,
  But – O God! that I came alone!

We dwell in peace, my beautiful one
  And I, by the streams of the West,
But oft through the mist of my dreams along
Rides Bannerman of the Dandenong,
  With the blood-red rose on his breast.

H. P. ('DUKE') TRITTON (1886-   )

'Duke' Tritton is a retired shearer and old folk-song singer. He remembers many old bush-songs, including some not recorded from any other source; but he composed this song himself, with the help of a few work-mates. A few years ago he added the last two stanzas to the song 'to bring it up to date'.

Shearing in the Bar

My shearing days are over, though I never was a gun:
I could always count my twenty at the end of every run.
I used the old Trade Union shears, and the blades were running
    full
As I shoved them to the knockers and I pushed away the wool.
I shore at Goorianawa and never got the sack;
From Breeza out to Comprador I always could go back;
But though I am a truthful man I find, when in a bar,
That my tally's always doubled but – I never call for tar!

Now shearing on the Western Plains, where the fleece is full of
    sand
And clover-burr and cork-screw grass, is the place to try your
    hand;
For the sheep are tough and wiry where they feed on the Mitchell
    grass,
And every second one of them is close to the 'cobbler' class;
And a pen chocked full of 'cobblers' is a shearer's dream of hell,
And loud and lurid are their words when they catch one on the
    bell:
But when we're pouring down the grog you'll hear no call for
    tar,
For the shearer never cuts them – when he's shearing in a bar!

At Louth I got the bell-sheep, a wrinkly tough-woolled brute,
Who never stopped his kicking till I tossed him down the 'chute.
Though my wrist was aching badly, I fought him all the way:
I couldn't afford to miss a blow – I must earn my pound a day;

So when I took a strip of skin, I would hide it with my knee –
Gently turn the sheep around so the right bower couldn't see,
Then try to catch the rousy's eye, and softly whisper, 'Tar';
But it never seems to happen – when I'm shearing in a bar!

I shore away the belly-wool, and trimmed the crutch and hocks,
Then opened up along the neck, while the rousy swept the locks,
Then smartly swung the sheep around, and dumped him on his
    rear –
Two blows to chip away the wig – (I also took an ear!)
Then down around the shoulder and the blades were opened
    wide,
As I drove them on the long blow and down the whipping side;
And when I tossed him down the 'chute he was nearly black
    with tar,
But it never seems to happen – when I'm shearing in a bar!

Now when the season's ended and my grandsons all come back
In their *Vanguards* and their *Holdens* – I was always 'on the
    track' –
They come and take me into town to fill me up with beer,
And I sit on a corner-stool and listen to them shear:
There's not a bit of difference! It must make the angels weep,
To hear a mob of shearers in a bar-room shearing sheep;
The sheep go rattling down the race and there's never a call for
    tar,
For they still don't seem to cut them – when they're shearing in
    a bar!

Then memories come crowding and they roll away the years,
And my hands begin to tighten and they seem to feel the shears:
I want to tell them of the sheds, of sheds where I have shorn,
Full fifty years, or maybe more, before the boys were born.
I want to speak of Yarragreen, Dunlop or Wingadee,
But the beer has started working and I find I cannot see.
So I'd better not start shearing – I'd be bound to call for tar;
Then be treated like a blackleg – when I'm shearing in a bar!

VII

(1870-   )

TOWN BALLADS

ALTHOUGH many bush songs were made as parodies of British street-ballads of the nineteenth century, there is not much evidence of a native street-balladry in Australia. If street-ballads were composed and sold in the first half of the last century none of them seem to have survived. There are, however, a few Australian broad-sheets surviving from the 1860s onwards, and a prolific street-ballad monger named 'Percy the Poet' certainly peddled his wares in Sydney as late as the 1930s. A few of them were taken up into oral tradition and are still sung, or recited, in different versions by people who have never heard of Percy.

We have included here too a few samples of 'literary' ballads which deal sympathetically, not to say sentimentally, with low life in the cities. Such verse became popular during and after the First World War, just at the time when bush balladry began to decline in popularity.

ANON

This old ballad celebrates one of the last old-fashioned, bare-knuckle prize-fights fought in Australia. The match took place in the open air at George's River near Sydney on 28 March 1871, before a large crowd of Irish and Scottish-descended partisans of the two principals. The ballad was first published and sung by a certain M. J. Conlon, copies being sold for threepence each; but whether Conlon also composed the song is not clear from the records.

Larry Foley, the winner, was regarded for long afterwards as Australia's champion pugilist. He opened a gymnasium in which he coached many young boxers and became a popular publican on his retirement.

The Orange and the Green

John Davies hears with great regret,
  The news that's going around,
That Sandy Ross has lost the fight
  At Georges River ground.
No more his crowing will be heard
  No more his colours seen,
For I think he's had enough this time,
  Of Foley and the green.

Chorus:
Oh, the green the colour of the brave,
  We'll raise high in the air,
And to our enemies we'll show
  The colour that we'll wear.
For the orange flag has been pulled down,
  The battle fought out keen,
And Sandy Ross has lost the fight
  At Georges River Green.

The yellow ties they mustered strong,
  Upon that Tuesday morn.
Poor Sandy he came up to time
  With his head and beard all shorn.
His yellow scarf around his waist
  Was plainly to be seen,
When Foley stepped into the ring
  To fight for Ireland's green.

'Sinn fein, sinn fein,' he cried aloud
  As he saw his friends close by,
'I've come to fight for Ireland's cause
  And for that cause I'll die.
And to deny her colours
  I ne'er will be so mean,
For in this ring I'll die or win
  For dear Old Ireland's green.'

'Here's to him men, here's to him boys,'
  Then Sandy Ross did say:
'I've come to fight for old King Bill
  Upon this glorious day.
My yellow scarf around my waist
  That has come into bud,
Will be dyed deep red upon this ground
  With this poor Fenian's blood.'

They both shook hands; you'd really think
  No ill-feeling lay between
The colours bright that made this fight,
  The Orange and the Green.
For two long hours that fight did last,
  Till Ross's seconds came between,
And threw the sponge high in the air,
  In favour of the green!

LOUIS ESSON (1879-1943)

Born in Edinburgh, Esson emigrated to Australia as a boy with his parents. He wrote plays and novels as well as verse, earning his living for most of his life as a freelance journalist.

Esson has here reproduced the argot of city larrikins of the period. Thus 'cray' (crayfish) is rendered phonetically as 'cr'y', 'today' as 'ter-d'y' and so on. Most other expressions which may be strange to the reader will be found listed in the Glossary.

Jugger's Out Ter-d'y

Give the push the office,
    Pass the 'at erlong,
Won't the Flyin' Angels
    'Ave er dance and song!
We've er busker organ,
    Beer, an' crimson cr'y,
Won't we blow the froth orf!
    Jugger's out ter-d'y.

Jugger got er sixer,
    Toppin' orf er John,
Stoushed 'im wi' er bottle,
    Back o' Little Lon.
Wen they tried ter bluff 'im
    Give the push aw'y,
Swore blind 'e never seen us,
    Jugger's out ter-d'y.

Won't them 'awkers edge it
    Wen 'e passes now!
Not er shutter lifted
    Since they jugged 'im. Yow!
Not er decent mix-up
    Since 'e went aw'y.
Won't it nark the rozzers!
    Jugger's out ter-d'y.

All the tarts iz waitin',
　　Linin' Little Lon,
In their flashest clobber,
　　Battlin' ter git on.
Floss and Mag and Clara –
　　Won't the feathers fly
Wen 'e picks the winner!
　　Jugger's out ter-d'y.

Watch the Johns go steady,
　　'E's the bloke to fite,
'E's the peb, gorblime,
　　Blow eround ter-nite.
Sling yer 'arf-er-dollar,
　　Tords the beer an' cr'y,
It's up to us to do 'im proud,
　　Jugger's out ter-d'y.

C. J. DENNIS (1876-1938)

Born in Auburn, a South Australian country town, Dennis spent
most of his life working as a journalist in Melbourne. Some-
times dubbed 'the Laureate of the Larrikin', his humorous verses
were tremendously popular during and after World War I. In
this passage Bill, the 'Sentimental Bloke', takes his girl, Doreen,
to a performance of *Romeo and Juliet*.

At the Play
(from *The Sentimental Bloke*)

'Wot's in a name?' she sez . . . An' then she sighs,
An' clasps 'er little 'ands, an' rolls 'er eyes.
'A rose,' she sez, 'be any other name
Would smell the same.
Oh, w'erefore art you Romeo, young sir?
Chuck yer ole pot, an' change yer moniker!'

Doreen an' me, we bin to see a show –
The swell two-dollar touch. Bong tong, yeh know.
A chair apiece wiv velvit on the seat;
A slap-up treat.
The drarmer's writ be Shakespeare, years ago,
About a barmy goat called Romeo.

'Lady, be yonder moon I swear!' sez 'e.
An' then 'e climbs up on the balkiney;
An' there they smooge a treat, wiv pretty words
Like two love-birds.
I nudge Doreen. She whispers, 'Ain't it grand!'
'Er eyes is shinin'; an' I squeeze 'er 'and.

'Wot's in a name?' she sez. 'Struth, I dunno.
Billo is just as good as Romeo.
She may be Juli-er or Juli-et –
'E loves 'er yet.
If she's the tart 'e wants, then she's 'is queen,
Names never count . . . But ar, I like 'Doreen!'

A sweeter, dearer sound I never 'eard;
Ther's music 'angs around that little word,
Doreen! . . . But wot was this I starts to say
About the play?
I'm off me beat. But when a bloke's in love
'Is thorts turns 'er way, like a 'omin' dove.

This Romeo 'e's lurkin' wiv a crew –
A dead tough crowd o' crooks – called Montague.
'Is cliner's push – wot's nicknamed Capulet –
They 'as 'em set.
Fair narks they are, jist like them back-street clicks,
Ixcep' they fights wiv skewers 'stid o' bricks.

Wot's in a name? Wot's in a string o' words?
They scraps in ole Verona wiv the'r swords,
An' never give a bloke a stray dog's chance,
An' that's Romance.
But when they deals it out wiv bricks an' boots
In Little Lon, they're low degraded broots.

Wot's jist plain stoush wiv us, right 'ere today,
Is 'valler' if yer fur enough away.
Some time, some writer bloke will do the trick
Wiv Ginger Mick,
Of Spadger's Lane. *E'll* be a Romeo,
When 'e's bin dead five 'undred years or so.

Fair Juli-et, she gives 'er boy the tip.
Sez she: 'Don't sling that crowd o' mine no lip;
An' if you run agin a Capulet,
Jist do a get.'
'E swears 'e's done wiv lash; 'e'll chuck it clean.
(Same as I done when I first met Doreen.)

They smooge some more at that. Ar, strike me blue!
It gimme Joes to sit an' watch them two!
'E'd break away an' start to say good-bye,

An' then she'd sigh
'Ow, Ro-me-o!' an' git a strangle-holt,
An' 'ang around 'im like she feared 'e'd bolt.

Nex' day 'e words a gorspil cove about
A secret weddin'; an' they plan it out.
'E spouts a piece about 'ow 'e's bewitched:
Then they git 'itched . . .
Now, 'ere's the place where I fair git the pip!
She's 'is for keeps, an' yet 'e lets 'er slip!

Ar! but 'e makes me sick! A fair gazob!
'E's jist the glarsey on the soulful sob,
'E'll sigh and spruik, an' 'owl a love-sick-vow –
(The silly cow!)
But when 'e's got 'er, spliced an' on the straight
'E crools the pitch, an' tries to kid it's Fate.

Aw! Fate me foot! Instid of slopin' soon
As 'e was wed, off on 'is 'oneymoon,
'Im an' 'is cobber, called Mick Curio,
They 'ave to go
An' mix it wiv that push o' Capulets.
They look fer trouble; an' it's wot they gets.

A tug named Tyball (cousin to the skirt)
Sprags 'em an' makes a start to sling off dirt.
Nex' minnit there's a reel ole ding-dong go –
'Arf round or so.
Mick Curio, 'e gets it in the neck,
'Ar rats!' 'e sez, an' passes in 'is check.

Quite natchril, Romeo gits wet as 'ell.
'It's me or you!' 'e 'owls, an wiv a yell,
Plunks Tyball through the gizzard wiv 'is sword,
'Ow I ongcored!
'Put in the boot!' I sez. 'Put in the boot!'
''Ush!' sez Doreen . . . 'Shame!' sez some silly coot.

Then Romeo, 'e dunno wot to do.
The cops gits busy, like they allwiz do,
An' nose around until 'e gits blue funk
An' does a bunk.
They want 'is tart to wed some other guy.
'Ah, strike!' she sez. 'I wish that I could die!'

Now, this 'ere gorspil bloke's a fair shrewd 'ead.
Sez 'e 'I'll dope yeh, so they'll *think* yer dead.'
(I tips 'e was a cunnin' sort, wot knoo
A thing or two.)
She takes 'is knock-out drops, up in 'er room:
They think she's snuffed, an' plant 'er in 'er tomb.

Then things gits mixed a treat an' starts to whirl.
'Ere's Romeo comes back an' finds 'is girl
Tucked in 'er little coffing, cold an' stiff,
An' in a jiff,
'E swallows lysol, throws a fancy fit,
'Ead over turkey, an' 'is soul 'as flit.

Then Juli-et wakes up an' sees 'im there,
Turns on the water-works an' tears 'er 'air,
'Dear love,' she sez, 'I cannot live alone!'
An' wiv a moan,
She grabs 'is pockit knife, an' ends 'er cares . . .
'*Peanuts or lollies!*' sez a boy upstairs.

ANON

This anonymous popular song may evoke in the minds of some readers comparisons with the English *Vicar of Bray*. It dates from the second decade of the present century and reflects the cynicism felt by some Australians towards the new nation's politicians – and their view of the benefits which compulsory arbitration of industrial disputes would bring to working men.

Bump Me Into Parliament

Come listen, all kind friends of mine,
　　I want to move a motion;
To make an eldorado here,
　　I've got a bonzer notion.

Chorus:

Bump me into Parliament,
　　Bounce me any wa---y.
Bang me into Parliament,
　　On next election day.

Some very wealthy friends I know
　　Declare I am most clever.
While some may talk for an hour or so,
　　Why, I can talk for ever.

I know the Arbitration Act
　　As a sailor knows his 'riggins':
So if you want a small advance
　　I'll talk to Justic Higgins.

Oh yes I am a Labor man,
　　And believe in revolution;
The quickest way to bring them on
　　Is talking consitution.

I've read my library ten times through,
   And wisdom justifies me.
The man who does not vote for me,
   By Cripes he crucifies me!

Chorus:

So bump 'em into Parliament,
   Bounce 'em any way;
Bang 'em into Parliament,
   Don't let the Court decay.

ANON

This anonymous soldiers' song of the First World War circulated in many versions, not all as urbane in tone as this one which was still being sung in the Second World War.

The Digger's London Leave

He went up to London and straight away strode
To Army Headquarters in Horseferry Road,
To see all the bludgers who dodge all the strafe,
By getting soft jobs on the Headquarters staff.

Chorus:
Dinky Di, Dinky di,
By getting soft jobs on the Headquarters staff.

A lousy lance-corporal said, 'Pardon me, please;
You've mud on your tunic and blood on your sleeve;
You look so disgraceful that people will laugh,'
Said the lousy lance-corporal on the Headquarters staff.

Chorus:
Dinky Di, Dinky di,
Said the lousy lance-corporal on the Headquarters staff.

The digger just shot him a murderous glance;
He said, 'We're just back from the shambles in France,
Where whizzbangs are flying and comforts are few,
And brave men are dying for bastards like you.'

Chorus:
Dinky Di, Dinky di,
And brave men are dying for bastards like you.

'We're shelled on the left and we're shelled on the right,
We're bombed all the day and we're bombed all the night.
If something don't happen, and that mighty soon,
There'll be nobody left in the bloody platoon.'

Chorus:
Dinky Di, Dinky di,
There'll be nobody left in the bloody platoon.

The story soon got to the ears of Lord Gort,
Who gave the whole matter a great deal of thought;
He awarded the digger a V.C. and two bars
For giving that Corporal a kick in the arse.

Chorus:
Dinky Di, Dinky di,
For giving that Corporal a kick in the arse!

'Percy the Poet', whose real name was apparently P. F. Collins, composed, published, and sold his own street-ballads in Sydney during the 1920s and 1930s. Some of them, like *The Death of Les Darcy* and *Phar Lap*, passed into oral tradition and have been recorded in different versions as far afield as North Queensland. Learned critics have been known to carp at Percy's prosody, but none have denied his patriotism or that he was possessed by the true *furor poeticus*.

Les Darcy is probably still Australia's most famous pugilist. While still in his early twenties he went to seek greater laurels in the United States but died there, despite the ballad's passionate asseverations to the contrary, probably of pneumonia.

Some fifteen years later Australia's most famous racehorse, Phar Lap, met a similar fate. His heart is preserved in the national Institute of Anatomy at Canberra and his stuffed hide stands in a glass case to greet visitors just inside the main entrance to the Melbourne museum.

The Death of Les Darcy

In Maitland cemetery
Lies poor Les Dar-cy,
His mother's pride and joy,
Australia's bonny boy.
How we long for the night
Just to see Les Darcy fight –
   How he beat 'em,
   Simply eat 'em,
Every Saturday night!

Chorus:

There lies young Les Darcy,
   Who we know was so ill-advised.
When the sad news reached us,
   How the tears stood in our eyes.

His one great ambition
　　Was to fight at the Golden Gate,
But the Voice that called him from us
　　Proved to be the sad hand of Fate!

The critics by the score
Said they had never saw
A lad like him before
Upon the Stadium floor.
Oh the Yanks thought him a skiter,
But he proved himself a fighter –
　　So they killed him,
　　Yes they killed him,
In Memphis Tennessee!

Phar Lap
(To the memory of Phar Lap, the world's greatest horse.)

He was a mighty horse indeed,
　　Alas: he's passed away;
But the world will remember him
　　Until the latest day.
Robert the Divil was a steed
　　Whose name will ever shine.
Another name will live in fame –
　　The famous Carbine.

They forced Phar Lap to do too much.
　　That much we know quite well.
What caused his death when in his prime,
　　The future may yet tell.
He closed his eyes in Yankee-land,
　　Of every evil thing;
And there Les Darcy passed away.
　　A champion of the ring.

His speed was wonderful, no doubt;
  His staying power was great;
It's very sad that he should meet
  With such a tragic fate.
He was the marvel of the age,
  The swiftest beast on earth:
New Zealand loved his Lightning name --
  The land that gave him birth.

Australia too was proud of him,
  This land of sun and shine:
For Telford and his partner
  He was a rich gold mine.
Pike tells us that he knew his work,
  His temper was perfect:
In fact, some say he was possessed
  Of Human intellect.

Five hundred years may come and go
  Before another's bred
To equal that swift noble steed
  Now numbered with the dead.
But if a man did poison him
  May his flesh and blood decline,
May his grave be made on a mountain side
  Where the sun will never shine!

Why Women Rule the Men

In days of old as we've been told
  The women ruled the men.
The men like fools did make new rules
  And ruled them back again!
But womenkind were not content,
  They wanted the franchise:
The world is topsy-turvy now,
  And that is no surprise.

They now play hockey and football
   And some can run and jump;
And tabbies who do hate these sports
   Would give a man the hump.
There are many men now in gaol,
   Their wives wont let them out:
The women now do boss the roost,
   They do without a doubt.

Some females in the labour cause
   Have got great intellect;
They have a system of their own,
   And that is most perfect:
Another class of womenkind
   Do now wear the trousers,
And some are almost off their dot
   Listening to the wowsers.

Outside the Children's Court one day,
   One Catherine O'Byrne,
Shot a false man, one Gibbs by name,
   As dead as a red herring:
But take all women, good and bad,
   There is this much about them,
To keep this world as it is
   We cannot do without them.

The Power of a Banana

Adam and Eve in the garden sat,
   They had no cause to hurry –
But something in the mind of Eve,
   Caused her to sigh and worry.
When she got up and walked about,
   As handsome as Diana;
Then Adam said to her, my dear,
   Do have a ripe Banana.

Chorus:
Banana, Banana,
Ripe and sweet Banana.
If your wife is cross with you,
Just give her a Banana.

They were as happy as could be,
    And free from earthly care;
They were allowed to eat all fruits,
    Except one apple rare –
But the Devil came, just like a snake,
    Some say like a goanna.
Then Adam ate the apple rare,
    And Eve had a Banana.

A friend of mine two years ago,
    Met with a lovely girl.
Her golden hair and large blue eyes
    Would fascinate an Earl.
She's now his wife and happy too,
    Her name it is Johanna –
She's proud of him, why so, because
    He gave her a Banana.

Sure, fruit is good at any time,
    'Twill make one strong and healthy,
The King, the Queen, the soldier brave,
    The poor, likewise the wealthy.
There's Peaches, Pears, and Passion-fruit:
    When next you meet Susanna –
Don't be shy, wink your left eye,
    And give her a Banana.

ANON

TWO NED KELLY SONGS

These anonymous folk-songs gained currency during and after the Second World War. The first invokes Ned's memory to help in driving back the Japanese invaders. The second is a wry comment on the war-time and post-war inflation.

Ned Kelly Was a Gentleman

Ned Kelly was a gentleman:
  Many hardships did he endure.
He battled to deprive the rich
  Then gave it to the poor.
But his mode of distribution
  Was not acceptable to all,
Though backed by certain gunmen
  Known as Gilbert and Ben Hall.

I think it was a pity
  They hanged him from a rope.
They made Australian history
  But they shattered Kelly's hope.
If they'd sent him into Parliament
  His prospects would be bright.
He'd function for the masses
  If not for the elite.

And perhaps now in Australia
  We'd have millions trained with him,
All laughing with a vengeance
  At the little yellow men.
If Ned and such guerillas
  Were with us here today
The Japs would not be prowling round
  New Guinea and Milne Bay.

Since Ned went over the Border
   There has been many a change,
Yet we may adopt his tactics
   Around the Owen Stanley Range.
Poor Ned, he was a gentleman
   But never understood.
We want men of such mettle now
   To stem the yellow flood!

The Ned Kelly Song

Ned Kelly was born in a ramshackle hut,
   He'd battled since he was a kid:
He grew up with bad men and duffers and thieves,
   And learnt all the bad things they did.

Now down at Glenrowan they held up the pub,
   And were having a drink and a song,
When the troopers rolled up and surrounded the place;
   The Kellys had waited too long.

Some say he's a hero and gave to the poor,
   While others, 'A killer,' they say;
But to me it just proves the old saying is true,
   The saying that crime doesn't pay.

Yet, when I look round at some people I know,
   And the prices of things that we buy;
I just think to myself, well perhaps, after all,
   Old Ned wasn't such a bad guy.

VIII

CONTEMPORARY POETRY

Most of the poems in this section are not ballads at all and not even particularly popular verse of any sort. We have sought rather to give from the work of some of the most considerable living Australian poets, a few poems which suggest how deeply the ethos of the ballads has coloured Australian life and culture. Such poets as FitzGerald, Slessor, Wright, Martin, Dutton, Thiele, Manifold, Campbell, Stewart, and Hope feel no need, as the balladists usually did, consciously to stress the Australianness of their work: yet many of the attitudes to life which were stated by the balladists have been subsumed and taken for granted, not repudiated, by these later and larger singers.

We have included also two or three ballads, genuine as any, but written in recent years.

R. D. FITZGERALD (1902-   )

Born in Sydney and educated at Sydney Grammar School, FitzGerald comes of an old Australian family which has long been prominent in literary and cultural life. A surveyor by profession, he has published nine books of verse.

In this poem he remembers an ancestor who was present at the flogging of some Irish rebel convicts in 1800.

The Wind at Your Door

My ancestor was called on to go out –
a medical man, and one such must by law
wait in attendance on the pampered knout
and lend his countenance to what he saw,
lest the pet, patting with too bared a claw,
be judged a clumsy pussy. Bitter and hard,
see, as I see him, in that jailhouse yard.

249

Or see my thought of him: though time may keep
elsewhere tradition or a portrait still,
I would not feel under his cloak of sleep
if beard there or smooth chin, just to fulfil
some canon of precision. Good or ill
his blood's my own; and scratching in his grave
could find me more than I might wish to have.

Let him then be much of the middle style
of height and colouring; let his hair be dark
and his eyes green; and for that slit, the smile
that seemed inhuman, have it cruel and stark,
but grant it could be too the ironic mark
of all caught in the system – who the most,
the doctor or the flesh twined round that post?

There was a high wind blowing on that day;
for one who would not watch, but looked aside,
said that when twice he turned it blew his way
splashes of blood and strips of human hide
shaken out from the lashes that were plied
by one right-handed, one left-handed tough,
sweating at this paid task, and skilled enough.

That wind blows to your door down all these years.
Have you not known it when some breath you drew
tasted of blood? Your comfort is in arrears
of just thanks to a savagery tamed in you
only as subtler fears may serve in lieu
of thong and noose – old savagery which has built
your world and laws out of the lives it split.

For what was jailyard widens and takes in
my country. Fifty paces of stamped earth
stretch; and grey walls retreat and grow so thin
that towns show through and clearing – new raw birth
which burst from handcuffs – and free hands go forth
to win tomorrow's harvest from a vast
ploughland – the fifty paces of that past.

But see it through a window barred across,
from cells this side, facing the outer gate
which shuts on freedom, opens on its loss
in a flat wall. Look left now through the grate
at buildings like more walls, roofed with grey slate
or hollowed in the thickness of laid stone
each side the court where the crowd stands this noon.

One there with the officials, thick of build,
not stout, say burly (so this obstinate man
ghosts in the eyes) is he whom enemies killed
(as I was taught) because the monopolist clan
found him a grit in their smooth-turning plan,
too loyally active on behalf of Bligh.
So he got lost; and history passed him by.

But now he buttons his long coat against
the biting gusts, or as a gesture of mind,
habitual; as if to keep him fenced
from stabs of slander sticking him from behind,
sped by the schemers never far to find
in faction, where approval from one source
damns in another clubroom as of course.

This man had Hunter's confidence, King's praise;
and settlers on the starving Hawkesbury banks
recalled through twilight drifting across their days
the doctor's fee of little more than thanks
so often; and how sent by their squeezed ranks
he put their case in London. I find I lack
the hateful paint to daub him wholly black.

Perhaps my life replies to his too much
through veiling generations dropped between.
My weakness here, resentments there, may touch
old motives and explain them, till I lean
to the forgiveness I must hope may clean
my own shortcomings; since no man can live
in his own sight if it will not forgive.

Certainly I must own him whether or not
it be my will. I was made understand
this much when once, marking a freehold lot,
my papers suddenly told me it was land
granted to Martin Mason. I felt his hand
heavily on my shoulder, and knew what coil
binds life to life through bodies, and soul to soil.

There, over to one corner, a bony group
of prisoners waits; and each shall be in turn
tied by his own arms in a human loop
about the post, with his back bared to learn
the price of seeking freedom. So they earn
three hundred rippling stripes apiece, as set
by the law's mathematics against the debt.

These are the Irish batch of Castle Hill,
rebels and mutineers, my countrymen
twice over: first, because of those to till
my birthplace first, hack roads, raise roofs; and then
because their older land time and again
enrolls me through my forbears; and I claim
as origin that threshold whence we came.

One sufferer had my surname, and thereto
'Maurice,' which added up to history once;
an ignorant dolt, no doubt, for all that crew
was tenantry. The breed of clod and dunce
makes patriots and true men: could I announce
that Maurice as my kin I say aloud
I'd take his irons as heraldry, and be proud.

Maurice is at the post. Its music lulls,
one hundred lashes done. If backbone shows
then play the tune on buttocks! But feel his pulse;
that's what a doctor's for; and if it goes
lamely, then dose it with these purging blows –
which have not made him moan; though, writhing there,
'Let my neck be,' he says, 'and flog me fair.'

One hundred lashes more, then rest the flail.
What says the doctor now? 'This dog won't yelp;
he'll tire you out before you'll see him fail;
here's strength to spare; go on!' Ay, pound to pulp;
yet when you've done he'll walk without your help,
and knock down guards who'd carry him being bid,
and sing no song of where the pikes are hid.

It would be well if I could find, removed
through generations back – who knows how far? –
more than a surname's thickness as a proved
bridge with that man's foundations. I need some star
of courage from his firmament, a bar
against surrenders: faith. All trails are less
than rain-blacked wind tells of that old distress.

Yet I can live with Mason. What is told
and what my heart knows of his heart, can sort
much truth from falsehood, much there that I hold
good clearly or good clouded by report;
and for things bad, ill grows where ills resort:
they were bad times. None know what in his place
they might have done. I've my own faults to face.

JUDITH WRIGHT (1915-   )

Born on a station near Armidale, New South Wales, Judith
Wright comes from an old Australian pioneering family. She is
by common consent one of Australia's most considerable poets,
is married (Mrs J.P. McKinney) and has one daughter.

The 'Country Town' of the poem's title is Armidale.

Country Town

This is no longer the landscape that they knew,
the sad green enemy country of their exile,
those branded men whose songs were of rebellion.
The nights were cold, shepherding; and the dingoes
bawling like banshees in the hills, the mist coming over
from eastward chilled them. Beside the fire in the hut
their pannikin of rum filled them with songs
that were their tears for Devonshire and Ireland
and chains and whips and soldiers. Or by day
a slope of grass with small sheep moving on it,
the sound of the creek talking, a glimpse of mountains,
looked like another country and wrenched the heart.
They are dead, the bearded men who sang of women
in another world (sweet Alice) and another world.

This is a landscape that the town creeps over;
a landscape safe with bitumen and banks.
The hostile hills are netted in with fences
and the roads lead to houses and the pictures.
Thunderbolt was killed by Constable Walker
long ago; the bones are buried, the story printed.

And yet in the night of the sleeping town, the voices:
This is not ours, not ours the flowering tree.
What is it we have lost and left behind?
Where do the roads lead? It is not where we expected.

The gold is mined and safe, and where is the profit?
The church is built, the bishop is ordained,
and this is where we live: where do we live?
And how shall we rebel? The chains are stronger.

Remember Thunderbolt, buried under the air-raid trenches.
Remember the bearded men singing of exile.
Remember the shepherds under their strange stars.

Born at Orange, New South Wales, Slessor was educated at Sydney Church of England Grammar School. He is one of Australia's most distinguished journalists and war-correspondents, a member of the Commonwealth Literary Fund Advisory Board, and a co-editor of the *Penguin Book of Modern Australian Verse*.

Country Towns

Country towns, with your willows and squares
And farmers bouncing on barrel mares
To public-houses of yellow wood
With '1860' over their doors,
And that mysterious race of Hogans
Which always keeps General Stores. . . .

At the School of Arts, a broadsheet lies
Sprayed with the sarcasm of flies:
'The Great Golightly Family
Of Entertainers Here Tonight'
Dated a year and a half ago,
But left there, less from carelessness
Than from a wish to seem polite.

Verandas baked with musky sleep,
Mulberry faces dozing deep,
And dogs that lick the sunlight up
Like paste of gold – or, roused in vain
By far, mysterious buggy-wheels,
Lower their ears, and drowse again. . . .

Country towns with your schooner bees,
And locusts burnt in the pepper-trees,
Drown me with syrups, arch your boughs,
Find me a bench, and let me snore,
Till, charged with ale and unconcern,
I'll think it's noon at half-past four!

A Bushranger

Jackey Jackey gallops on a horse like a swallow
Where the carbines bark and the blackboys hollo.
When the traps give chase (may the Devil take his power!)
He can ride ten miles in a quarter of an hour.

Take a horse and follow, and you'll hurt no feelings;
He can fly down waterfalls and jump through ceilings,
He can shoot off hats, for to have a bit of fun,
With a bulldog bigger than a buffalo-gun.

Honeyed and profound is his conversation
When he bails up Mails on Long Tom Station,
In a flyaway coat with a black cravat,
A snow-white collar and a cabbage-tree hat.

Flowers in his button-hole and pearls in his pocket,
He comes like a ghost and he goes like a rocket
With a lightfoot heel on a blood-mare's flank
And a bagful of notes from the Joint Stock Bank.

Many pretty ladies he could witch out of marriage,
Though he prig but a kiss in a bigwig's carriage;
For the cock of an eye or the lift of his reins,
They would run barefoot through Patrick's Plains.

THOMAS V. TIERNEY (1882-1959)

Born at Bungaree near Ballarat, Victoria, Tierney worked in the bush for most of his life but lived in Melbourne for twenty years or so prior to his death. He published two books of verse and was a foundation member of the Melbourne *Bread and Cheese Club*.

Rafferty Rides Again

There's a road outback that becomes a track
Where the hills dip down to the plain;
And on misty moonlight nights up there
The old inhabitants all declare
On his big black stallion (or was it a mare?)
Rafferty rides again.

A bushranger bold in the days of old,
'Twas an evil name that he bore,
Till they shot him down from behind a tree –
At least that's the yarn they told to me
When I asked who this Rafferty bloke might be,
And what he was riding for.

And it now appears, after all the years
That low in his grave he has lain,
That o'er the hills, in the same old way,
Dashing and debonair, reckless, gay,
On his chestnut charger (or was it a bay?)
Rafferty rides again.

I have waited long the old hills among,
But my vigils have been in vain;
I've perched all night in a towering tree,
But devil a ride he'd ride for me,
Though I would have given the world to see
Rafferty ride again.

But the tale is true that I'm telling you,
Though it's ages since he was slain;
To all the folk in the hills 'tis known
That, awesome and spectral, and all alone,
On his snow-white courser (or was it roan?)
Rafferty rides again.

EDWARD HARRINGTON (1895-   )

Born at Shepparton in Victoria, Ted Harrington once described himself in conversation as a 'literary throw-back'. He served abroad in the Australian Light Horse during the First World War and tried his hand at farming and many other jobs afterwards. He was one of the last writers whose verses all remain completely within the bush-ballad tradition of the eighteen-nineties.

The Bushrangers

Four horsemen rode out from the heart of the range,
Four horsemen with aspects forbidding and strange.
They were booted and spurred, they were armed to the
    teeth,
And they frowned as they looked on the valley beneath,
As forward they rode through the rocks and the fern –
Ned Kelly, Dan Kelly, Steve Hart and Joe Byrne.

Ned Kelly drew rein and he shaded his eyes –
'The town's at our mercy! See yonder it lies!
To hell with the troopers!' – he shook his clenched fist –
'We will shoot them like dogs if they dare to resist!'
And all of them nodded, grim-visaged and stern –
Ned Kelly, Dan Kelly, Steve Hart and Joe Byrne.

Through the gullies and creeks they rode silently down;
They stuck-up the station and raided the town;
They opened the safe and they looted the bank;
They laughed and were merry, they ate and they drank.
Then off to the ranges they went with their gold –
Oh! never were bandits more reckless and bold.

But time brings its punishment, time travels fast –
And the outlaws were trapped in Glenrowan at last,
Where three of them died in the smoke and the flame,
And Ned Kelly came back – to the last he was game.

But the Law shot him down (he was fated to hang),
And that was the end of the bushranging gang.

Whatever their faults and whatever their crimes,
Their deeds lend romance to those faraway times.
They have gone from the gullies they haunted of old,
And nobody knows where they buried their gold.
To the ranges they loved they will never return –
Ned Kelly, Dan Kelly, Steve Hart and Joe Byrne.

But at times when I pass through that sleepy old town
Where the far-distant peaks of Strathbogie look down
I think of the days when those grim ranges rang
To the galloping hooves of the bushranging gang.
Though the years bring oblivion, time brings a change,
The ghosts of the Kellys still ride from the range.

The Swagless Swaggie

This happened in the years gone by before the bush was cleared,
When every man was six foot high and wore a heavy beard;
One very hot and windy day along the old coach road,
Towards Joe Murphy's wayside pub a bearded stranger strode.

He was a huge and hairy man well over six foot high,
An old slouch hat was on his head and murder in his eye;
No billycan was in his hand, no heavy swag he bore,
But deep and awful were the oaths that swagless swaggie swore.

They were a rough and ready lot, the bushmen gathered there,
But every man was stricken dumb to hear that stranger swear;
He cursed the bush, he cursed mankind and all the universe,
It froze their very blood to hear that swagless swaggie curse.

'I met the Ben Hall gang,' he said, 'the bastards stuck me up,
They pinched me billy, pinched me swag, they pinched me flamin'
    pup;

They turned me pockets inside out and took me only quid,
I never thought they'd pinch me pipe, but s'elp me God they did.

'I never done the gang no harm, I thought 'em decent chaps,
But now I wouldn't raise a hand to save 'em from the traps;
I'm done forever with the bush, I'm makin' for the town,
Where they won't stick a swaggie up and take a swaggie down.'

The bushmen were a decent lot, as bushmen mostly are,
They filled the stranger up with beer, the hat went round the bar;
The shearers threw some blankets in to make another swag,
The rousers gave a billycan and brand new tucker bag.

Joe Murphy gave a briar pipe he hadn't smoked for years,
The stranger was too full for words, his eyes were dim with tears;
The ringer shouted drinks all round, and then to top it up,
The shearers' cook, the babbling brook, gave him a kelpie pup.

Next day an hour before the dawn, the stranger took the track,
Complete with pup and billycan, his swag upon his back;
Along the most forsaken roads, intent on dodging graft,
He headed for the great north-west, and laughed and laughed
    and laughed.

Born Ludwig Detsinyi in Hungary, David Martin was educated
in Berlin and experienced the first years of Nazi rule. He fought
for the Spanish Republic as a volunteer first-aid man in the
International Brigade and later lived in Britain for about ten
years. In 1947 he went to India as a journalist. With his family,
he settled in Australia in 1949.

These two poems, which body forth the very essence of Aus-
tralian attitudes to life in a way that has been equalled by few
native-born writers, suggest his poetic stature.

Jack Underwood

Jack Underwood I'm writing on,
A bushman. He is dead and gone;
Jack Underwood is gone.
At Putty Hill he was shot dead
By some mischance, straight through the head,
That's how his death was won.
At Putty Hill, straight through the head.
Down by the creek they made his bed,
And there he sleeps alone,
But still he's more alive than most
Who ride the bush with their own ghost
Following close upon.
Many there are who still recall
How Jack all night in Putty Hall
Like some mad demon danced,
And how he laughed, and how he sang,
And how he made his banjo twang
Till girls like trout in summer sprang
And lads like brumbies pranced.
At flood time, or when men turn out
To build a dam against the drought,
His name falls on your ear:
'Seems heavy work without poor Jack,
My word, I wish we had him back,
He could do everything, our Jack,

I wish we had him here.'
Or when the races come around,
And thunder rises from the ground,
And when the field's away,
Someone is sure to say:
'I wish poor Jack was riding there,
With him about 'twas fair and square,
He could do everything, old Jack:
Wish he was riding there.'
When lies the party-line inflame
To poison honest women's fame,
Until the most endearing name
Is 'interfering fool,'
Or when the Progress meeting bogs,
And cousins snarl like hungry dogs,
Someone will cry: 'Keep cool!
For shame! what are we, beasts or men?
That's not how Jack would do it!' Then
One after one they'll grin:
'If you are half as good, go on
And tell us how to do it, son;
Jack could do everything: come on,
We'll back you, place or win.'
There is a ring, a special ring,
About this word, this *everything*
That Jack, they say, could do:
As if the spirit of the place
Had suddenly assumed a face,
The cheerful dial of our race,
Indomitably new!
And so in Putty to this day
Jack Underwood still makes his way
As if he had not died,
And Tom, his son, takes after him,
A bush boy, soft of speech and slim,
And bold, and steady-eyed.

Bush Christmas

Stuffed with pudding to his gizzard
  Uncle James lets out a snore,
Auntie Flo sprawls like a lizard
  On the back verandah floor.

Grandpa Aub sits with a flagon
  On the woodheap 'neath the gums,
And he thinks he's seen a dragon
  Where the pigs are munching plums.

Cousin Val and Cousin Harry,
  Cousin May and Cousin Fred,
Play the goat with Dulce and Larry
  By the creek below the shed.

In the scrub the cows are drowsing,
  Dogs are dreaming in the shade.
Fat and white, the mare is browsing,
  Cropping softly, blade by blade.

It is hot. Mosquitoes whirring.
  Uncle James rubs his knee:
'Flo,' he whispers, 'are you stirring?
  It's near time to get the tea.'

GEOFFREY DUTTON (1922-   )

Member of a pioneer South Australian pastoral family, long
prominent in that state's history, Dutton was educated at Gee-
long Grammar School, Victoria, and Oxford University. He
served in the Royal Australian Air Force during the war and is
married, with three children. Dutton has published three books
of verse, a novel, travel-books, biography and criticism.

Wool-shed Dance

The dust shaken and stamped from their feet
Is red as autumn in the rain-soft south
Where leaves by boot and hoof are mashed
And mingled in the grass, and vine-roots
Slip as surely into the dark earth
As an arm into a sleeve. A trace of it clings
Still in the cracks of their bouncing boots
As the saltbush and myall to their crumbled ground.
The air, heavy with the smell of wool,
Leans to a lamp by an empty bench
From the wool-bales of watchers, the non-dancers,
As the floor slopes down to the open
Double doors where the lamp makes yellow
The posted night. The jigging shadows
Ripple on the corrugated wall with the dancers,
Heel and toe in a clacking polka,
And a sturt pea on a faded dress
Burns like the black heart of autumn.
The accordeon squeezes a new tune
And peg-leg waltzes with a ten-months baby,
Beer to ballast his wooden knee,
And the mother is proud that it does not cry.
A bottle rings on the earth like a stone
And the cook finds a tortuous path
To bed, like a myall root through rocks
Winding heavy and dark as iron.
Past midnight in the brightest moonlight

The lights will grow black and go out,
Till sober and drunks go home,
And each year the seasons, like the accordeon,
Squeezed in the cracked hands of the earth,
Play the same tune over and over again
To grey saltbush on the red land,
While in the south the rainwet trees
Strip boughs as bare as roots for winter.

COLIN THIELE (1920-   )

Born at Eudunda, South Australia, Thiele graduated in Arts at the University of Adelaide, served in the Royal Australian Air Force during the War, and now lectures in English at the Wattle Park Teachers' College, South Australia. In addition to books of poetry he has written for Radio many verse-plays and other features.

Country Pubs

Each four-square limestone monument
Of praise to man's heroic thirsts
Heaves elementally and bursts
With gusty, shirt-sleeved merriment.

And though verandahs loll and sprawl
Or windows arch their lidless eyes,
And leaning posts apostrophise
The unsafe step and sagging wall,

Yet Spring in street and paddock hurls
Its sap till every corner brims,
And morning jumps along the limbs
Of singing trees and ready girls.

With breasts and buttocks firm as trees
The barmaid-waitress blooms and sways;
And drinking timber-men appraise
How thighs grow upwards from the knees;

All day they dream and climb astride
Such satin-smooth and supple forks,
And cling and linger in their talks
Of stems so straight and scarfs so wide;

And tractor-drivers' glances state
That doors they know of have no locks
And love wears deftly-zippered frocks
When sudden Spring and moonlight mate.

And shearers ask for leg and tart:
No matter what the table lacks
These come to them as midnight snacks,
Kept hot and served with lusty art.

And in the bar and Men's redoubt
Gargantuan drinkers handle beer
With massive feet apart, and steer
It grandly in or grandly out.

Australia Fair pursues its way,
And in its myth of malt and mirth
The nation's salt still goes to earth
On each up-country Saturday.

Of an old pastoral family, Campbell was born on a station near
Adelong, New South Wales. He was educated at the King's
School, Parramatta, and at Cambridge University where he
graduated in Arts. He played football for England against Ire-
land and Wales and won a D.F.C. and bar as a pilot in the
Royal Australian Air Force during the War.

No living poet surpasses Campbell in evoking the essence of
past Australian experience of the land itself.

Song for the Cattle

> Down the red stock route
> Hock-deep in mirage
> Rode the three black drovers
> Singing to the cattle.

> And with them a young woman,
> Perhaps some squatter's daughter
> From homestead or township,
> Who turned her horse easily.

> To my mind she was as beautiful
> As the barmaid in Brewarrina
> Who works at the Royal. Men
> Ride all day to see her.

> Fine-boned as a brigalow
> Yet ample as a granary,
> She has teeth good for laughing
> Or biting an apple.

> I'm thinking of quitting
> My mountain selection,
> The milking at morning
> And the lonely axe-echoes;

Of swapping my slab hut
For a rolled-up blanket
And heading north-westward
For a life in the saddle –

For the big mobs trailing
Down the empty stock routes,
A horned moon at evening
And songs round the campfire.

Yes, I'll soon be drinking
At the Royal in Brewarrina
And ambling through mirage
With the squatter's daughter.

Hogan's Daughter

Clancy saddles his narrow mare
    For frosts have come before the rain,
And he's away with Conroy's sheep
    To drove them on the western plain.

He whistles an old dog to the lead,
    A roan kelpie to crowd the rear;
And whistles a song to suit himself
    As rose-hips dance on the winter brier.

And they string along a drover's mile
    And dust is ringing from the shale
When lightning skins the bony ridge
    And green as opal falls the hail.

And they string along a drover's mile
    When granite heights stand up on air;
The lightning lights on Hogan's pub
    And a long girl knitting behind the bar.

'O what is the web you weave, girl?
    What is the net you knit so thin
That blows with the lamp and your yellow hair?'
    'It's a web to catch a drover in.

'The winds are loose in the mountain sky
    And tear the fleece from the fleeing storm;
Tether your mare or ride on by,
    Here's a fire to wrap your spirit warm.'

His mare is hitched to the veranda rail;
    In long green paddocks stray the sheep,
The dogs are barking in the hall –
    And he has kissed her underlip.

'Is it mirage-water brims your eye
    Or a spring where a man may drink his fill?'
The lightning clove the cliffs of sky;
    He stood alone upon the hill.

Then good-bye to his dark lank wife
    And his shack and his shears and his family;
And drought or the devil take Conroy's sheep
    And the hips that dance on the brier-tree.

For he rolled a swag of his saddle-cloth
    And called his kelpie dogs to heel,
Fixed his eye on the glinting storm;
    And he has gone across the hill.

Harry Pearce

I sat beside the red stock route
And chewed a blade of bitter grass
And saw in mirage on the plain
A bullock wagon pass.
Old Harry Pearce was with his team
'The flies are bad,' I said to him.

The leaders felt his whip. It did
Me good to hear Old Harry swear,
And in the heat of noon it seemed
His bullocks walked on air.
Suspended in the amber sky
They hauled the wool to Gundagai.

He walked in Time across the plain,
An old man walking in the air,
For years he wandered in my brain;
And now he lodges here.
And he may drive his cattle still
When Time with us has had his will.

JOHN MANIFOLD (1915-   )

Born in Melbourne and educated at Geelong Grammar School,
Victoria, Manifold graduated in Arts at Cambridge. He served
with the British Army in Africa and Europe during the War.
Married, with two children, he has been living for some time in
Queensland.

His ancestors were amongst the first squatters in the Western
District of Port Phillip, later the state of Victoria, and his work
shows a deep feeling for traditional Australian values. An
accomplished musician as well as a poet, he has done much work
in the field of Australian folk-songs and ballads, and is the editor
of *The Penguin Australian Song Book*.

Chillianwallah Station

When his hopes of a colonelcy faded away
He retired to the colonies, still on half-pay;
Preferring to Cheltenham a Gulf-country run
And a heat of a hundred-and-ten in the sun.

His cook was a Cantonese – Asian at least! –
Who thought enough curry as good as a feast;
And his ex-soldier-servant, from Antrim, named Barney,
Used to rowse the black stockmen in bad Hindustani.

He kept the fair flag of the Empire afloat
By wearing a tunic done up to the throat;
And the style of his most conversational speeches
Had its thumbs well in line with the seam of its breeches.

He played a straight bat, and a good hand at solo,
He would ride forty miles for a chukker of polo,
So the district forgave him his finical pride
Which demurred for so long at selecting a bride.

Then the seasons got worse, and the banks took a hand,
They called in the mortgage they held on his land;
And the Major was found in the harness-room, shot
Thro' the head with his old-fashioned Webley-&-Scott.

The jury said: 'Accident; no one's to blame,'
And the Major was buried, leaving only the name
'Chillianwallah' in letters some eight inches high
On the gate of the stock-route to remember him by.

Except that old Barney's the grandfather now
Of a quarter-cast family, no one knows how,
Who have never been coached since the Major passed on
But who ride like the Ashtons and bat like the Don.

Bogong Jack and the Trooper

There's a story told about Bogong Jack
    And I won't go bail it's true,
But I ran across it a few years back
    And I'll pass it along to you.

He wasn't in Kelly's class, of course,
    Nor a hero like Brave Ben Hall,
But he couldn't resist a beautiful horse
    Branded or not: that's all.

This kept the traps in a state of strain
    From Omeo clear to Bright,
Till the squatters murmured they'ld not complain
    If Bogong were shot at sight.

A constable on his promotion once
    Attempted to do just that
When he sighted his man by the merest chance
    A mile above Clover Flat.

At the range it was probably hopeless; still
   It made his intention clear.
So Bogong belted away up hill
   With the trap not far in rear.

He went for the Kiewa Fork like smoke
   Where the creeks ran high with the rains,
For he reckoned the trap was a willing bloke
   But his mount might show more brains.

Smash through the water went Bogong Jack
   And patted his mare's wet skin,
But the trooper's horse at the brink shied back
   And the trooper went right in.

You shouldn't go into those mountain creeks
   Unless you're a mountain trout,
For it may be a matter of days or weeks
   Before anyone hauls you out.

Well, the trooper wasn't. He simply clung
   To a rock with either hand,
And whenever the water bared his tongue
   He called upon Jack to 'stand'.

'Stand?' says Jack. 'I'ld be grateful to,
   For it's been an exhausting game;
But its hardly the thing for me to do
   When you can't do the same!

'Are you going to be long in there? If so,
   I'll just have a bite and sup
From the saddlebag here. I should like to know
   How long you can keep it up.'

The trap gave in. He'd begun to feel
   Like one of an angler's worms,
So he kicked the boot from each waterlogged heel
   And accepted Bogong's terms.

He let his belt and his pouches drift
   And settled himself to swim
On the blown-up waterbag – thoughtful gift –
   Which Bogong handed him.

Bogong rode for a mile or more
   On the bank as he floated down,
Poling him carefully off from shore
   And seeing he didn't drown.

The trooper got home all right, it's said,
   But resigned from the Force next day;
And his boots are down on the Kiewa's bed,
   And there I suppose they'll stay.

This story may be a lot of tripe,
   But if that's so it's odd
That I once found a rowell of Government type
   In the craw of a Murray cod.

DOUGLAS STEWART (1913-   )

Born and educated in New Zealand, Douglas Stewart came to
Australia in 1938 and was for some twenty years chief literary
editor and art critic of the Sydney *Bulletin*. He is a member of
the Advisory Board of the Commonwealth Literary Fund. He
has published several collections of poems, but is perhaps best
known for his poetic dramas, *Ned Kelly*, *The Fire on the Snow*,
The Golden Lover, and *Shipwreck*.

The Adaminaby of the poem's title was an old bush township
in the Australian Alps. Since World War II it has been submerged
beneath an artificial lake, constructed as part of the huge Snowy
River Scheme for generating hydro-electricity and irrigating arid
country on the inland plains to the west.

The Man from Adaminaby

Hard to say where he came from –
   Maybe the Great Divide
Where the sun like a golden raindrop
   Rolls down Kiandra side.

Or down from Kelly's high plains
   With his pick-axe over his shoulder
Or out of a hollow snowgum
   Or out of a granite boulder –

Or maybe he came from Bugtown
   That's far enough out and further,
Though there isn't any town at Bugtown
   And there aren't any bugs there either.

Anyway on his white horse
   He rode down out of the hills,
His pick-axe over his shoulder,
   His two black dogs at his heels.

– 'A long way back to Kiandra,
  Miles further than you'd think,
Where the mullock-heaps glint on the hillside
  And the white snow-daisies wink;

'A long way back to Kiandra
  Over the blue sky's brink
But here's old Adaminaby
  Where a man can get a drink.

'Cool are the bar and the beer there,
  And my old mates gathered round' ...
– 'You'll wait a long time for a drink, mate,
  The blooming pub's been drowned.'

– 'Seen a high tide myself there,
  The beer right up to our necks' ...
– 'She's sunk like a ship, we tell you,
  With all the rest of the wrecks.

'Where have you been these years
  With your mare and your dogs and your pick?
The whole town's under the water,
  Pisé and stone and brick.

'While you were sinking your shaft, mate,
  Or shearing, was it, or droving,
They shut the old pub right down, mate,
  They brought in early-closing.

'The publican, none too soon,
  Has finally lost his licence;
Chimney and shadowy door there
  Drink to each other in silence.

'Only the shag like a copper
  Dives down to the window to peer;
Yabbies crawl over the counter,
  Mud-eyes are into the beer.

'At the bar door the bunyip
   Lies down and scratches his fleas:
And a great wave of the Snowy
   Says "Time, gentlemen, please."

'There's drink enough still of a kind, mate,
   If your taste runs as far as water,
It's over the cafe, too mate,
   It's over the tallest poplar.

'But the beer she's off for ever
   And so is Adaminaby,
It's all under water making
   Hydroelectricity.'

– 'Hydroelectricity
   Don't make no sense to me
And there's the whole town still standing
   So far as I can see.

'It runs right down to the farms there
   Under the shining air
And pink the apple-trees bloom there,
   Like a white cloud the pear.

'She's the old town as ever
   And all my mates will remember me
When I go down as always
   To drink in Adaminaby.'

– 'She's drowned, she's gone, she's flooded!'
   – 'Ah, tell the marines,' he cried,
And called his black dogs to him
   And spurred the white mare's side,

And rode on down the hillside
   As he had done for years
And straight out under the water
   And drank there with his peers.

A. D. HOPE (1907-   )

Born at Cooma, now the headquarters of the Snowy Scheme in New South Wales, Hope was educated at Fort Street High School, Sydney, and later at Sydney and Oxford Universities. He is married with three children and is now the Professor of English in the Australian National University, Canberra.

He is one of the most considerable, and certainly one of the most versatile, of all Australian poets; but a satirical attitude, a sardonic tone, and a contempt for all forms of cant and affectation underlie most of his work. It may be no more than an accident that these qualities, in an unsophisticated form, also characterize so much Australian balladry.

Toast for a Golden Age

Ebrius haec fecit terris, puto, monstra Prometheus:
Saturnalicio lusit er ipse luto.

Martial.

Here's to you, all of you, objects of fun or resentment,
Hail-fellow gentlemen, friends, wherever you are!
Sitting at ease with your arm round ten stone of contentment,
Or treating your favourite ulcer with gin at the bar.

Leading the story-book life of the fabulous biped,
The Male Cinderella, the fairy godmother's chum;
When Father Bear growled: 'There is somebody lying in *my*
      bed!'
You laughed in his face or gave him a kick in the bum.

And here you are living happily ever after
And buying a round of drinks to prove that you are,
Or holding the blonde in the moonlight helpless with laughter
At your line of talk in the parked expensive car.

You were born with hair on your chest and a voice like thunder,
You said: Bang, Bang, Bang! and everyone fell down dead:
All of your life you found, and little wonder,
The girls kept climbing in and out of your bed;

All of your life it was you who were asked to the party;
When the ship went down, it was you were saved from the wreck;
You slept like a top, you were fit and cheerful and hearty
And most of your troubles were solved by writing a cheque.

Your trousers were pressed, your well-bred, civilized features
Appeared in the press and everyone knew that face –
And that is why the committee of living creatures
Toasts you tonight as type of the human race.

For tonight is an anniversary celebration
By all the beasts of modest intelligence
For the pensive ape who invented civilization
And lived on his wits at the rest of the world's expense.

Tonight we celebrate the triumphs of reason
And the rational animal's most remarkable feat:
The way he contrives, in season and out of season,
To solve the problem of getting too much to eat.

For the Earth, our mother, at last has found a master:
She was slow and kindly, she laughed and lay in the sun –
Time strapped to his wrist, he made the old girl work faster,
Stripping her naked and shouting to make her run.

He chopped the mantle of pines from her beautiful shoulders,
He ripped her breasts for his vines, her belly for corn;
And she smiled and grew green again and did as he told her,
And trebled the bounty of her plenteous horn.

Till the soil grew parched and thin, and the famine followed;
So he broke new ground – but he bred as the locust bred –
The acres he sowed by day were always swallowed
By the rivers he sowed at night in his double-bed.

He cracked his stock-whip: that characteristic gesture
Made dust of the plains and the hurricane bore it away.
A thousand years had gone to making the pasture
Which the wind or the flood destroyed in a single day.

And that is why, though we understand tonight you
Are otherwise engaged, and we do not mind,
Your fellow creatures had chosen to invite you
As a representative specimen of your kind.

Not one of the masters of the human spirit,
But the common denominator of the mass;
Not the giver of grace or wisdom all inherit,
But a middle-aged, middle-brow male of the middle-class.

We would not like you to think, your friends are jealous;
Their turn may come; they have waited since time began.
But if man is the measure of all things, as you tell us,
All things from you may take the measure of man.

So we wait and watch you, and feel the planet grow colder,
The deserts grow larger – it's no use making a fuss –
We wait for the day when Time, speaking over your shoulder,
Remarks that the dog-in-the-manger has missed the bus;

When the heir to the silver spoons and the winning tickets
Has a pain inside him and suddenly loses his hair;
And he gropes in his heart, in his hat, in his fourteen pockets,
But the ticket is missing – the ticket has never been there.

Glossary

of obsolete or colloquial Australian words and expressions

Alluvial: Easily mined gold, usually found on or near the surface of the ground.

Ashtons: A pastoral family which includes many champion polo-players.

Baal Gammon: Aboriginal pidgin='You're not joking'?

Bandicoot: A species of small marsupials.

Bangalow: A native palm-tree.

Barcoo: A watercourse, in the far west of Queensland.

Barcoo rot: A kind of scurvy.

Barmy: Eccentric or insane.

Barramundi: A Queensland fresh-water fish.

Battler: A poor man, game, honest but creditably unsuccessful.

Billabong: A pond, strictly an ox-bow lake formed by the anabranch of a river.

Billy or *billy-can:* A tin fitted with a wire handle and used primarily for making tea.

Bligh: Governor of New South Wales from 1806 to 1808 when he was deposed by a rebellion of the military garrison.

Blow: 1. A single stroke of the shears. 2. To boast.

Blue: 1. To squander a cheque. 2. A fight or brawl.

Board: The floor of a shearing-shed.

Bob: Shilling.

Bobby: Policeman.

Bogan Gate: A low pass in the western Blue Mountains.

Boobook: A mopoke (q.v.).

Boomer or *boomah:* An unusually large, full-grown kangaroo; hence anything big.

Bosker or *busker:* Splendid.

Bower, Right Bower: The superintendent or boss of a shearing-shed. (From the card-game of Euchre).

Box: A species of eucalypt.

Boxed: Mixed. Used when different mobs of sheep, or other stock, mix together.

Breaker: One who breaks-in horses.

Brolga: A large native crane, sometimes called the Native Companion.

Brumby: A wild horse.

Budgery: Aboriginal pidgin='Good on you'!, or 'Good for you'!

Bulletin: Once the best-known weekly journal in Australia, strongly radical and nationalist in tone.

Bunyip: A mythical and monstrous beast, believed by many early settlers to inhabit water-courses and swamps.

Bushranger: An Australian highwayman or bandit.

Cabbage-tree: A broad-brimmed hat made from the plaited fronds of the native cabbage-tree palm.

Castle Hill: A penal settlement for twice-convicted felons.

China or *China Plate:* Mate (rhyming slang).

Chink or *Chinkie:* A Chinese.

Chow: A Chinese.

Chuck: Throw.

Chute or *Shoot:* A sloping runway down which sheep make their way out of the shed after they have been shorn.

Cleanskin: An unbranded calf, hence one peculiarly liable to be stolen.

Cliner or *clinah:* Girl.

Clobber: Clothing.

Cobber: Mate, close friend.

Cobbler: The last sheep left in the pen when the bell rings to mark the end of a day's work. Hence, a sheep which is very difficult to shear.

Cockatoo or *Cocky:* Usually a small-scale farmer. Earlier, sometimes, an ex-prisoner from Cockatoo Island Gaol, Sydney Harbour.

Coo-ee: An Aboriginal hail or call, borrowed by the early settlers and still used to make contact with persons at a distance in the bush.

Coolibah: A species of eucalypt.

Cop: Policeman.

Cornstalk: A white native of New South Wales.

Cove: Man, fellow: sometimes, master or boss.

Cradle: An appliance in which water was rocked with ore to separate it from the gold.

Cronk: Disreputable, out of order.

Crook: Bad or sick: as a noun=a criminal.

Crow-eater: A South Australian.

Cruster: Policeman.

Cuddy: A horse.

Cup, the: The Melbourne Cup, trophy for the winner of Australia's most famous horse-race.

Currency Lad or *Lass:* In the early days, a native-born Australian, usually of convict stock.

Cut out: 'The sheds were all cut out' – Shearing was finished.

Damper: Bush bread. A large 'loaf' of flour and water, kneaded together and cooked by placing it on a bed of glowing embers and then raking more embers over it.

Darcy, Les: Most celebrated of Australian boxers who died in his prime during World War I in the United States.

Darling Pea: A poisonous native plant which drives stock mad.

Darling, Sir Ralph: Governor of New South Wales 1825-31. During his term of office convict discipline was made more severe.

Depôt: A Hostel in Sydney for the shelter of unattached female immigrants.

Dewdrop: An axe.

Digger: 1. A gold-digger. 2. An Australian soldier – equivalent to 'Tommy' or 'GI. Joe'.

Diggins: The (Gold) Diggings – the gold-fields.

Dingo: The Australian native wild dog.

Dinkum or *dinky-di(e):* True, genuine, or authentic.

Dogger: A dingo-trapper.

Domain: Sydney's open-air forum for orators, equivalent to London's Hyde Park.

Don, the: Sir Donald Bradman, the Australian cricketer.

Dopey: Stupid.

Duff: 1. A bush pudding, tied in a cloth and boiled. 2. To steal (stock); a cattle-duffer=a cattle-thief.

Duke: One who excels, a natural leader.

Edge it: Funk it: walk on the edge of the pavement to avoid the possibility of a quarrel.

Emu Plains: A penal settlement for twice-convicted felons.

Eureka: Site of the only 'battle' fought on Australian soil when gold-diggers clashed with soldiers and policemen on 3 December 1854.

Factory or *female factory:* A house of correction for refractory female convicts.

Fall: A whip thong.

Fan: To 'frisk' or search.

Flash: Showy, boastful, cheap.

Fluke: A disease of sheep.

Flyin' Angels: A Melbourne 'push'.

Footrot: A disease of sheep.

Gazob: Fool.

Gidgee: A small tree, sometimes growing very thickly.

Gin: An adult female Aborigine.

Glassey or *glassy:* Exact copy; 'to be the glassy on'=to be the very image of.

Goanna: A large lizard; name probably derived from iguana.

Gorblime: Corruption of 'God blame me!'

Government Stroke: A slow or lazy manner of performing work. Originally from the reputed working habits of 'Government men' or convicts.

Graft: Hard work.

Gully-raking: Cattle or stock-stealing.

Gun: An expert or champion shearer.

Higgins: A radical middle-class politician, later first President of the Federal Arbitration Court.

Hogget: A yearling sheep.

Holden: The commonest brand of motor-car in Australia today.

Hopping Colonel, The: Lieut-Colonel Henry Dumaresq, brother-in-law of Governor Darling and his private secretary, later Commissioner for the Australian Agricultural Company in Australia. As the result of a wound sustained at Waterloo, Dumaresq limped badly.

Howe, Jacky: The champion blade-shearer of all time.

Humping the drum or *the swag,* or *bluey,* etc.: Carrying one's bundle of camping-gear, i.e. tramping through the bush.

Humpy: A shanty.

Hunter: Governor of New South Wales from 1795 to 1800.

Huts: Often=the working hands' quarters, as opposed to the 'House' or 'Homestead' of the squatter or his manager.

Hysonskin: Tea.

Iron-gang: A band of convicts set to work in irons and under strict discipline, usually on the roads.

Jackeroo or *jackaroo:* A young man, often of good family, who lives in the homestead with the squatter's or manager's family but works with the station-hands to gain experience.

Jenkins: An escaped convict, turned bushranger, hanged in Sydney in 1834 for the murder of Dr Wardell.

Joe, Jo: A policeman. More often a cry used to warn of the approach of police.

John: Policeman.

Johnny-cake: A flat cake of flour and water paste, toasted on a bed of glowing embers.

Jug: Prison; to jug=to put in prison.

Jumbuck or *jumbuk:* A sheep.

Kelpie: A breed of Australian sheep-dog.

King: Governor of New South Wales from 1800-1806.

Kip: Occasionally swag or tucker-box: Once a small, flat piece of wood with a square edge, used as a 'scriber' by timber-getters to mark the flat end of a felled tree-trunk for sawing into planks: Today usually the small flat piece of wood used for tossing the pennies in the (illegal) game of 'two-up'.

Knocking down (*a cheque*): See lambing down.

Lag: A convict. To lag=to arrest or convict.

Lambing-down: 1. The act of squandering a cheque; 2. *or of* despoiling another of his money by causing or enticing him to squander it on drink.

Lash: Fighting or brawling.

Leather-jack: A flat cake of flour and water paste, fried in a pan.

Little Lon: Little Lonsdale Street in Melbourne, long notorious for its brothels.

Logan, Captain P.: Commandant of Moreton Bay Penal Settlement 1826-30, murdered in the latter year by Aborigines said to have been prompted to the deed by the convicts.

Mallee: A species of eucalypt forming a thick scrub.

Matilda: A swag or bushman's bundle of belongings; hence, to waltz Matilda – to carry one's swag or tramp the roads.

Milne Bay: At the eastern extremity of New Guinea: site of the first defeat inflicted on Japanese land-forces during World War II.

Moke: A horse.

Moleskins: Serviceable cotton working trousers.

Moniker: Name.

Mopoke: A species of owl.

Moreton Bay: A penal settlement for the punishment of twice-convicted felons, established on the present site of Brisbane.

Murray: Australia's largest river.

Myall: 1. A tree found in semi-desert areas. 2. A wild Aborigine.

Nardoo: A native plant bearing edible seeds.

Nark: A spoil-sport; as a verb – to anger.

Native: Usually an Australian-born 'native white'. Less often an Aboriginal 'native black'.

New chum: A recently arrived immigrant.

Nit: To keep nit – to keep watch while one's confederates engage in some disapproved activity.

Norfolk Island: A penal settlement for twice-convicted felons.

Office: 'Give the office' – Pass the news.

Off-sider: A bullock-driver's mate who walked on the off-side of the team. Hence a mate or an assistant of any kind.

Old man (*Kangaroo*): A large, fully grown kangaroo.

Overlander: A long-distance drover, particularly one who makes inter-colonial journeys with stock.

Owen Stanley Range: The mountainous backbone of the island of New Guinea.

Paddy-melon: A small marsupial of the kangaroo family.

Paroo: A watercourse in western Queensland and N.S.W.

Peb: Pebble – the winner or leader.

Peckers: Keep up your peckers – keep up your spirits, cheer up.

Peeler: Policeman.

Picker-up: A rouseabout employed to pick up the fleeces from the floor while the shearers are at work.

Pike: Jockey of Phar Lap, most famous Australian race-horse.

Pimp: An informer. As a verb, to inform.

Plant: Hide, or something hidden.

Playing of the game: Engaging in prostitution.

Poking it: Poking borak, i.e. giving cheek, insulting.

Port Arthur: A Tasmanian penal settlement for twice-convicted felons.

Port Macquarie: A penal settlement for twice-convicted felons.

Pre-emptive right: A squatter's or pastoral lease-holder's right, under certain conditions, to buy portion of his lease at a fixed price.

Push: A band or gang of friends, especially of city larrikins.

Quid: Pound note.

Rhino: Money.

Ringer: A champion shearer: specifically, he who 'rings' the shed, i.e the shearer who shears the greatest number of sheep in a given shearing-shed.

Robertson, Jack: (Sir) John Robertson, a N.S.W. politician who took the leading part in passing the first Free Selection Act of 1861. He held that Australians should increase the population by their own domestic efforts.

Rocks, The: The oldest slum district in Sydney.

Rouseabout or *rousy:* A general handy-man, especially in a shearing-shed.

Rowse: To scold.

Rozzers: Policemen.

Rum: (as an adjective) Odd and perhaps questionable.

Rum-culls: Old mates in crime.

Run: A sheep or cattle-station. Sometimes a spree.

Sandy Blight: Ophthalmia.

Schooner: A large-sized beer-glass.

Selection: A small farm, or land for a farm.

Selector or *Free-selector:* A small farmer.

Shanty: A shack or hut; often – grog-shanty.

Shed: Often – shearing-shed.

Sheila: A girl.

Silvertail: A rich, fashionable, or well-bred person.

Skite: A boaster, or to boast.

Slab: A plank, split from the log and adzed by hand.

Smacker: A pound note.

Smooge: To 'pet' or make love.

Snagger: A clumsy shearer.

Snob: To snob was to mend shoes.

Snowy: The Snowy River, now the main waterway in a great national hydro-electric scheme.

Spell: A period of rest.

Spiel: 1. To talk glibly and unreliably. 2. To gallop or canter freely on horseback.

Spieler: A glib and garrulous cheat.

Splitter: One who fells and splits trees into shingles, fence-posts, or slabs of timber.

Sprag: To accost.

Spruiker: A glib and probably dishonest speaker, especially one who seeks to sell something; a side-show barker.

Squatter: A large-scale grazier.

Station: A large grazing estate, a ranch.

Store Cattle: Beasts which need to be 'stored' and fattened before sale.

Stoush: Fight (as noun or verb).

Stringy-bark: The bark of certain eucalypts, used to make bark huts, as kindling, and for many other purposes.

Sundowner: A tramp or itinerant bush-worker.

Super: A station superintendent.

Swag: Bundle of belongings and camping gear, slung from the shoulders

Swagman: A tramp or itinerant bush-worker.

System: The Convict System.

Talking Bullock: Swearing.

Tally: The number of sheep shorn by a shearer in a day's work.

Tank: Often – a depression in the ground scooped out for storing rain-water.

Tar-boy: In big sheds, when a sheep is cut during shearing, a tar-boy applies tar to the wound.

Tart: Girl or sweetheart.

Telford: Owner of Phar Lap, most famous Australian racehorse.

Ten: A common scale of rations in the bush was 'Tens' – ten pounds of flour, ten pounds of meat, and smaller amounts of sugar and tea per week.

Thunderbolt: Fred Ward, a celebrated bushranger of the New England district.

Toongabbee: A penal settlement for twice-convicted felons.

Topping off: Knocking out, or informing upon.

Trap: Policeman.

Triangle: A device to which convicts were trussed for flogging.

Tucker: Food.

Tug: A hardy person.

Twig: Understand.

Tyson (James Tyson): A millionaire squatter of the nineteenth century.

Vanguard: A popular modern motor-car.

Wallaby: A smaller species of kangaroo.

Wardell, Dr Robert: Journalist, lawyer, and newspaper proprietor, murdered by bushrangers in 1834.

Wet: Angry.

Whip the cat: To complain, repent, or bemoan one's fate.

Whipping side: The last side of a sheep to be shorn.

Wowser: A puritan or moralistic spoil-sport.

Yabby: A species of fresh-water crayfish.

Yeo: Ewe.

Index of Titles

Index of First Lines

Some more
Australian titles
are described on the
following pages

THE PENGUIN AUSTRALIAN
SONG BOOK

John Manifold, who has an international reputation as an authority on folk music and as a poet in his own right, has brought together a magnificent variety of words and music in *The Penguin Australian Song Book*. His material comes from traditional sources but is all alive today.

Some eighty songs are divided into the following sections: Seamen and Transports; Immigrants and Diggers; The Bushrangers; Pastoral Australia; The Nomads; The Poets.

The versions given are based on meticulous scholarship tested by public performance, and notes to each song are provided. These are the songs of a new nation, ready for singing by one or many voices.

FOUR AUSTRALIAN PLAYS

Although these plays are published for the first time, they have already been performed and acclaimed throughout Australia, and have arisen out of the theatre workshops that are beginning to be recognized as the source of the most exciting developments in local theatre for many years.

ALEXANDER BUZO

'. . . Somewhere in the forests of Mr Buzo's theatrical imagination there is a tiger, here felt rather than glimpsed in the snarl of an occasional line and the swipe of a paw in a confrontation, and I refuse to believe it a paper tiger.' H. G. Kippax. *Sydney Morning Herald*, August 1969

JACK HIBBERD

'It was at La Mama that I first saw the work of Jack Hibberd, a writer of sinister Pinteresque persuasion and potentially a great talent.' Phillip Adams, 1968

JOHN ROMERIL

'. . . The most promising work so far is the Van Itallie style play, *The Man from Chicago*, about delusions on the brink of madness—or, rather, a questioning of what sanity is today.' Katharine Brisbane, *Australian*, February 1970

With an introduction by Graeme Blundell

A NEW BRITANNIA

Humphrey McQueen

In writing his interpretative analysis of the components of Australian radicalism and nationalism in the nineteenth and early twentieth centuries, Humphrey McQueen has written a hard-hitting manifesto for the New Left. He describes his work as 'a frantic dash from one battlefield to another' in an attempt to demonstrate that nineteenth century Australia was a capitalist society and not possessed by some natural socialist ethos.

McQueen is perceptive and often amusing as he examines what he sees as the essentially racist character of Australian nationalism, our 'seige mentality', the workers' concern for property symbolized the piano, and the petit-bourgeois nature of the La Parties that emerged after 1890.

This book may well be attacked for being extreme but it will generate controversy and force its way into consideration wherever Australian history is being seriously discussed.

MORRISON OF PEKING

Cyril Pearl

In 1897 Dr George Ernest Morrison, a young Australian journalist, was appointed to the staff of the London *Times* as its Peking correspondent. He was soon to become the greatest and most influential foreign correspondent of his era.

In his youth Morrison walked the trail of Burke and Wills across Australia and explored unknown New Guinea.

Meticulously and judiciously drawing on Morrison's vast collection of papers and diaries, Cyril Pearl has written an authoritative, full-blooded and often witty biography of an extraordinary man whose life and achievements influenced the course of Chinese history at one of its most crucial periods.